PRACTICAL OUTDOOR SURVIVAL

PRACTICAL OUTDOOR SURVIVAL

••••

A MODERN APPROACH

Len McDougall

THE LYONS PRESS

Printed in the United States of America

Design by M.R.P.

10   9   8   7   6   5

Library of Congress Cataloging-in-Publication Data

McDougall, Len.
     Practical outdoor survival: a modern approach / Len McDougall.
       p.   cm.
     Includes index.
     ISBN 1-55821-228-0
     1. Wilderness survival.   I. Title.
GV200.5.M376 1993
613.6'9—dc20
                                      92-41783
                                          CIP

To Bill Shaw, my mentor and my friend.
You believed in me even when I thought
you were foolish for doing so. Thank you.

CONTENTS

INTRODUCTION

Before purchasing this book, one might ask, why another outdoor survival book? There are about a dozen wilderness survival books on the market at any given time, by such noted experts as Tom Brown and Bradford Angier.

But most read more like studies in ancient anthropology than working manuals on survival techniques. And isn't that what most folks in the market for an outdoor survival book really want —survival tips they can use? Few of the recreational outdoorsmen who lose their way—or their lives—in the woods are practicing students of outdoor survival. Most are sport hunters, many are weekend campers, and some are simply victims of unhappy circumstances—survivors of a light plane crash, for example.

For these people outdoor survival means doing what it takes to stay alive until they can get back to civilization. The canoeist who has just lost his vessel and all of his supplies to a stretch of killer rapids has no need to know how to tan a whitetail hide or fashion a stone spearhead, especially if he has a small survival kit in a buttpack or even a jacket pocket. He *does* need to know how to build an emergency shelter to weather a sudden storm or how to start a fire in the rain.

Knowing what to do in an emergency and how to do it is a large part of the science of outdoor survival. But so is preparation.

The reason a woodsman who finds himself in a survival situation doesn't need to know how to chip a cutting tool from a piece of obsidian is because he had the foresight to carry a good belt knife. Likewise, he doesn't need to know how to fashion rope from retted plant fibers if he thought to include a 100-foot package of parachute cord in his kit. I've always thought it ironic that a smoker often has a better chance of surviving in cold weather than the average non-smoker simply because he will always be carrying a lighter or matches.

Modern technology has afforded us many conveniences that our forefathers were denied, and it behooves us to make use of them. Even survivors of a nuclear holocaust would not regress to the Stone Age—they would still have vise-grip pliers, lag screws, and solar calculators. Engineers, doctors, and machinists would still remember their special skills and the knowledge of producing electricity from wind, water, and the sun would not be forgotten.

There's nothing "wimpy" about being prepared for an emergency in the wilderness. Anyone can dump a canoe, break an ankle, or get caught in a sudden snowstorm. It's utterly ridiculous to willingly venture into the wild without taking a reasonable selection of survival tools. The reason early Native Americans used stone, wood, and bone implements is because they had no alternative. When Europeans arrived, Native Americans discarded the bow and arrow in favor of the muzzle-loading rifle, and their stone knives for much stronger steel blades. And not many a northern woodsman would venture more than a few paces from his cabin without his trusty steel hatchet. Today, microelectronics and other technical innovations make it possible for the woodsman to be the best-equipped, most self-sufficient human being to ever enter the wilderness.

Thus, this book will cut through the mystique surrounding outdoor survival—much of it perpetuated by survivalists themselves—and present only the information the reader will need to get back home. It doesn't contain information about twisting fibers into a bowstring, fashioning deerskin garments, or cooking with wooden utensils. It does contain information about equipment, signaling aircraft, navigation, and staying healthy during an extended period in the wilderness. It will tell the reader how to build a shelter, skin game, start a fire in the rain, and find palatable, nutritious wild food. In short, it offers the would-be survivalist pertinent advice about how to stay alive until he can be rescued or find his way back to civilization.

Much of my own survival training was the result of growing up around the Ojibwa, Ottawa, and Chippewa Indians of northern Michigan. In those days there were still many old grandfathers who could recite the stories they'd been told by their own grandfathers and who were as comfortable speaking their own native languages as they were speaking English. There was nothing mystical about the experience ... they were just old fellows who enjoyed talking about the way life had been when they were growing up, and they in fact felt a moral obligation to pass along what they could of their vanishing culture. Most of the Indian children were more interested in the trappings and toys of the white man's world, but I absorbed every word the grandfathers told me. They taught me many survival skills, but the most valuable of these was the incredible way they taught me to see, hear, smell, and even feel the forest around me. Like them, I feel an obligation to pass along what I've learned, and for more than nine years I've taught wilderness survival to others, primarily teenagers. My methods sometimes differ from what I was taught because the modern woodsman has tools thay my Indian mentors didn't, but I like to think that this book will carry on the spirit of their teachings.

THE
SURVIVAL
KIT

one

"Be Prepared," the motto of the Boy Scouts of America, should be especially meaningful for anyone venturing into the wilderness to fish, camp, or hunt. Few recreational outdoorsmen actually believe they might come to harm in the woods. Like the lovely sirens who lured sailors to their deaths in Greek mythololgy, the beauty and grandeur of the wilderness often lulls human visitors into a false sense of safety.

And in fact, the wilderness is a very safe place, infinitely less hazardous than the roads and freeways we travel daily, and safer even than puttering around one's own home. Yet in my home state of Michigan alone the forests have claimed the lives of dozens of outdoorsmen over the past ten years. Some have never been found.

There's nothing insidious or evil about the dangers found in the woods. Dangers come from a lack of preparation. Each of us knows the type of terrain he will encounter during a trip in the wild. Whether one is flying in to a small Canadian lake, driving through Death Valley, or deer hunting in a large state forest, there's a wealth of modern, easily transportable survival items available to help survive the unforeseen. This chapter will deal with a number of the more important and useful items of survival, each with proven value as a survival tool.

Survival Knives

A strong, sharp knife is the woodsman's best friend. It's our solution to the problem of not having the teeth and claws our wilder cousins are endowed with. The survivalist's knife may be even more important to him than the natural tools and weapons of four-footed creatures. Without it, he'd have a tough time skinning prey, fashioning wooden implements, building shelters, or any of the other infinitely numerous chores that require the use of a blade.

Not all knives are created equal, and not all knives can qualify as honest-to-goodness survival knife, regardless of the name stamped on the blade. A true survival knife, designed to help keep its user alive under the most adverse conditions, bears little resemblance to that Buck Pathfinder Dad used for deer hunting. Neither does it look like the designer lawnmower blades used by Rambo or Crocodile Dundee. The former is too light and fragile, while the latter two are just too clumsy.

Utility and strength are the hallmarks of any survival knife. It must have a full tang—the portion of the blade that extends into the handle—for maximum strength. A knife with a full tang has a blade that is one solid piece from the tip to the butt of the handle. The design is standard for all GI-issue knives as well as high-quality civilian models.

A survival knife also has sawteeth cut into the back, or "spine," of the blade opposite the cutting edge. These are not designed to saw through branches, but to cut shallow, squared grooves into wood and bone. A shallow groove cut into two sides of a sapling will prevent a tied rope from sliding along its length, and sharp-sided notches are vital to the construction of quality snares and deadfalls.

The handle of a survival knife should always be contoured to fit its user's hand and should always have a grooved, checkered, or knurled surface. A smooth handle is slippery when wet or while the user is wearing gloves, making the knife hard to get a grip on and dangerous.

The knife should also have a wide fingerguard that extends beyond the blade in either direction. This will prevent the hand from sliding over the blade if a slip should occur. Fingerguards on some newer survival knives have flat and crosspoint screwdriver tips ground into either end.

The butt end of the handle should terminate in a solid, heavy, and firmly attached butt cap. The butt cap is meant to be used as a hammer, and must be equal to the task. One survival knife, the Imperial Schrade M-7S, has a unique buttcap that's squared on three sides for hammering and has a claw-type nail puller and ice claw on the fourth.

It's important that the blade have a "false" or unsharpened edge running two or three inches along the spine and down to the tip. The false edge isn't usually sharpened because its purpose is to penetrate rather than to cut. Having a false edge makes the blade terminate in a needle-like point, very useful for drilling holes in wood, bone, or leather.

Before purchasing a survival knife, give some consideration to the type of ground edge it has. Sharpness isn't important at this point, but the shape of the edge itself is. There are five basic edge types: saber-ground, flat-ground, hollow-ground, semi-hollow ground, and diamond-ground. The ground edge is what determines how strong the blade is and how sharp it can be made.

Until recently the sabre-ground edge was the standard for survival knives, military blades, and bayonets, and in general still is, although the new U.S. Army M9 Field Knife (made by Buck) has a semi-hollow ground edge. The saber-ground edge is shaped like a V, beginning about halfway down the blade and ending in a point at the cutting edge. It's difficult to sharpen because the entire surface of the ground edge must be honed down to make the point formed at the cutting edge sharp. It also dulls rather quickly regardless of how hard the steel is because the V formed by the edge is wide (the narrower the V, the sharper the edge).

The advantage of the sabre-ground edge is that the maker need remove only a minimal amount of material from the blade, leaving fully half of it at full thickness. The result is a blade that

SURVIVAL KNIFE EDGES

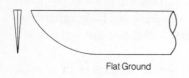

Flat Ground

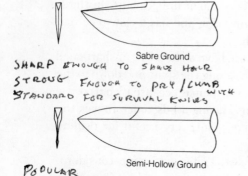

Sabre Ground

SHARP ENOUGH TO SHAVE HAIR
STRONG ENOUGH TO PRY/CLIMB WITH
STANDARD FOR SURVIVAL KNIVES

Semi-Hollow Ground

POPULAR
MUCH LIKE SABER GROUND

can, with practice and work, be made sharp enough to shave the hair off someone's arm while retaining enough brute strength to withstand the abuse of being used as a pry-bar, wedge, or climbing tool. The legendary Marine Corps K-Bar Fighting Knife and the USAF Pilot's Survival Knife have sabre-ground edges.

The flat-ground edge is similar to the V formed by the sabre-ground edge, except that it begins at the blade's spine and ends at the cutting edge, giving the entire blade a sharp V-shape. A flat-ground blade is necessarily wide in comparison to its thickness but can be honed to razor sharpness with little trouble and retains a functional cutting edge very well. It isn't as strong as the sabre-ground edge because more steel is removed when the edge is formed, but many an experienced woodsman has been willing to make the sacrifice. The Trailmaster, a large Bowie knife from the Cold Steel company, has a flat-ground edge, as do many folding knives.

The hollow-ground edge is the sharpest of them all. This is the edge found on straight razors and a few fillet knives. It's formed by grinding a wide groove along the length of the blade on either side, beginning at the spine of the blade and ending at the cutting edge. Unfortunately, so much metal is removed from the blade to form this edge that it becomes downright weak. Consequently, no companies are making a hollow-ground belt knife, and it's just as well.

The semi-hollow ground edge is another matter. This edge has such a strong following that it can be found on nearly every hunting knife ever made. It is formed by grinding a groove lengthwise along either side of the blade, much the same as the hollowground edge. The difference is that the semi-hollow ground edge has a much smaller radius, beginning only about halfway down the blade and ending at the cutting edge. This leaves half the blade at full thickness to maximize strength while narrowing the cutting edge into a sharp V that will take and hold a very keen honed edge. Because of the advent of superior alloys and heat-treating methods, this edge is gaining still more popularity among survivalists and professional woodsmen for whom a broken knife isn't just an inconvenience but a serious problem. The Gerber BMF Survival Knife, U.S. Navy UDT Knife, and the Buck M9 Field Knife have semi-hollow ground edges.

The last type of edge, the diamond-ground, is by definition unique to double-edge knives and daggers. Essentially a sabre-ground edge that has been duplicated on what would otherwise be the spine of the blade, it produces a second cutting edge; seen end-on the blade looks like a diamond. This edge cannot be made sharp and is inherently weak because so much metal is removed from the blade. Some manufacturers have attempted to improve the sharpness of the double-edge blade by giving it a shallow semi-hollow ground edge, but have only succeeded in further weakening the already anemic blade. Double-edge knives were created centuries ago to penetrate leather breastplates and fit between the links of chain-mail armor. Personally, I'd as soon carry a piece of sharpened flint as a double-edge knife in the woods.

The Bowie knife is a blade design usually associated with James Bowie, the American frontiersman, outlaw, and hero who died during the Battle of the Alamo in 1836. Some authorities credit creation of the distinctive blade to James' brother, Rezin Bowie, who reportedly came up with the pattern after nearly losing a thumb while fighting off a wild bull with his Green River trade knife.

BOWIE-TYPE SURVIVAL KNIFE

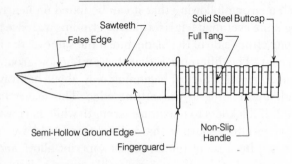

Regardless of which Bowie brother conceived it, the Bowie blade has become the basic style of nearly every hunting and survival knife made. The characteristics that distinguish the Bowie from other blade types are its wide, thick blade, good balance, heavy fingerguard, and long false edge. Its original use was as a weapon—a job for which it has proven itself well suited in several major wars—but the knife's solid design and intrinsic stoutness also make it a natural for survival work.

America saw its first hollow-handle survival knife in the 1974 movie *First Blood*, when Sylvester Stallone, an unappreciated Vietnam veteran, used it to make booby traps, slay a wild pig, navigate through the mountains, and generally make life miserable for a pompous sheriff, his minions, and the entire population of a small town in Washington state.

Today there are at least a dozen hollow-handle survival knives on the market, proof enough that the design has a following among outdoorsmen. At first glance it appears to be a wonderful idea to use the handle as a storage place for survival items—until one remembers that that's where the tang should be. Hollow-handle knives have no tang to speak of because the blade mounts to the handle rather than running through it. The design quite literally takes the backbone out of the knife, making it prone to breakage during hard use.

I suggest that anyone in the market for a serious survival knife that carries its own emergency items give some consideration to knives like the Imperial Schrade M-7S or Gerber BMF. Both of these offer the strength of a full tang and come with sheath pouches containing compass, matches, wire saw, and fishing tackle. Having said that, I recommend that anyone who still wants a hollow-handle knife purchase the Buckmaster made by Buck Knives.

The so-called "blood groove" still found on many blades, including the legendary K-Bar, should be avoided. In centuries past, when swords and large knives were standard infantry weapons, blood grooves were ground into either side of fighting blades to make them lighter and easier to manipulate. But they also remove a significant amount of strength from the blade.

Folding knives have little value as general-duty survival knives because, like hollow-handle knives, they have no tang. The blade is attached to the handle by a single pivot pin and held in the open position by a spring-loaded locking pawl or cam. The design is not a strong one, but it was never intended to be.

Still, the folding knife has a place in the survivalist's kit. The large size and brute stength of the general-duty survival knife, so desirable for building shelters, butchering large animals, and a host of other heavy chores, work against it during delicate tasks. Fashioning wooden implements and sensitive snare triggers and filleting fish are best accomplished by smaller, thinner blades. For these and many other light-duty chores I recommend any good 3-blade stockman's knife.

Selecting a survival knife is a lot like buying a car or a stereo, especially with the multitude of offerings on today's growing knife market. There are so many different brands, sizes, and styles of survival knives with so many different features in so many price ranges that choosing one can be a confusing experience. The following is a list of what I feel are the five best survival knives on the market today, based not on specifications and manufacturer's claims, but on hard experience. I've listed them in order of preference with their average retail price.

Imperial Schrade M-7S	$50.00	*Hollow Handle (semi hollow)*
USAF Survival Knife	$30.00	*Sabra*
Buck M9 Field Knife	$100.00	*semi hollow*
Gerber BMF	$150.00	*semi hollow (hollow handle)*
USMC Combat Knife	$40.00	*Sabra*

Survival Compasses

A compass is as important an item to have in the survival kit as a knife. While the knife is invaluable for helping the survivalist stay alive in the wilderness, a compass is just as valuable for helping him get back home.

Folks who have never learned to use a compass generally have the impression that learning to do so requires a college education. Not so. A compass simply points toward magnetic north. It points north all the time, every day, no matter which direction its owner is facing, and that's pretty much it. All of the other wonderful things that can be done using a compass are based on knowing where north lies and are performed by the user more than by the instrument.

Thanks to modern technology the woodsman of today can head into the wilderness carrying the most reliable and versatile portable land navigation system in history. Most have a rotating bezel marked to 360 degrees in increments of one degree, a built-in map scale marked in miles, kilometers, or both, a luminous needle or dial for night travel, and a highly accurate sighting system for zeroing in on prominent landmarks. The compass still just points north the way it has since the days of Columbus, but now it also has the measuring tools necessary to calculate distances, plot multidirectional courses or simply lead a confused hunter out of the woods.

In days gone by the air-filled compass was the only type available to navigators on land or sea. The air-filled compass is simply a magnetic dial or needle mounted on a pillar and enclosed in a case. The drawbacks of the design are that the compass will often stick in one place, collect condensation in wet weather, or freeze in cold weather. Any one of these problems can have serious consequences for the person in a survival situation, and I recommend avoiding the air-filled compass altogether.

Fortunately, the majority of quality-made compasses on the market are liquid-filled. Liquid-filled compasses generally have a very sensitive movement immersed in liquid and encased in a watertight housing. The liquid does nothing to impede the movement of the indicator as it rotates toward magnetic north, but it does provide a braking action to prevent the indicator from bouncing back and forth before settling, a problem common to cheaply made air compasses. The liquid will not freeze, even in subzero conditions, especially if the instrument is worn around the neck and inside the coat as it should be.

The biggest concern about the liquid-filled compass is that of durability. What if it springs a leak? The truth is that a leak is very nearly impossible, even under conditions of hard abuse. In my 23 years as both a teacher and student of wilderness survival only one liquid-filled compass has ever been damaged beyond use, and that occurred at home when my pit bull terrier decided to use it as a chew toy. Even without liquid the compass will still function—it just takes several seconds for the indicator to settle.

One problem that should be looked for when purchasing a compass is that of a bubble in the liquid. Small bubbles don't affect the movement of the indicator, but a large bubble can actually trap the needle and prevent it from pointing to magnetic north. Small bubbles can occur naturally in the field from the forces of expansion and contraction, but a bubble in a new compass is a pretty good indication that something went wrong at the factory.

One of the most popular compasses among hunters is the so-called "Hunter's Compass," a small, simple compass that pins onto the wearer's coat. Some are the dial type, some are spherical, and most are liquid-filled, but all of them should be avoided. I've lost count of the hunters who have told me about stopping to take a bearing only to discover that their compass was gone, ripped from their coats by a branch somewhere behind them.

Pocket compasses are simple compasses with an indicator needle or, more rarely, a rotating dial. Most aren't really intended to be carried in the pocket but worn on a lanyard around the neck. All quality pocket compasses are liquid-filled. Some have a rotating bezel marked to 360 degrees and a few have an integral carrying case with hinged cover.

Simple pocket compasses are somewhat limited because the map scales, sighting systems, and other tools found on more complex compasses have been sacrificed in the interests of economy. But don't get the idea that a pocket compass won't do the job. It may not be suitable for plotting a zig-zag course through mountains or deep swamp, but it is very much capable of leading a plane crash victim or stranded canoeist back to civilization along the most direct route.

The lensatic compass, a military design dating back to World War II, is considered by many to be the best compass available. It comes equipped with a rotating bezel marked to the nearest degree, folding front and rear sights for zeroing in on distant landmarks, and a built-in map scale. The entire unit is encased in a non-magnetic metal or plastic housing that folds into a compact package.

It's difficult fo fault a compass design that has proven its usefulness from the jungles of Okinawa to the desert of Iraq, but the lensatic compass has been forced to take a backseat to smaller and more versatile compasses in the last decade. Its only deficiencies are that it doesn't work as well with a map as some of the newer map compasses and its sighting system, so accurate for locating landmarks in open country, is nearly useless in the forest.

The map compass is the latest addition to the survivalist's orienteering arsenal. Official compass of the Boy Scouts and a favorite of professional woodsmen around the world, these highly versatile compasses are made of clear Plexiglas or high-impact plastic and, as the name implies, are specifically designed for use with a map. They have a rotating bezel for determining course direction to the nearest degree, map scales to determine distances in miles and kilometers, a liquid-filled housing, and a luminous indicator for night travel. The beauty of the map compass lies in its simple, uncomplicated design, durability, and versatility, all of which have strong appeal to the survivalist.

Like survival knives, there are many fine compasses on the market, all of which will perform admirably in any weather or terrain. Following is a list of what I consider to be among the best, again listed in order of preference.

Silva Type 3 Map Compass	$15.00
Silva Polaris Type 7	$10.00
Silva Trekker Type 20	$20.00
Silva Guide Type 26	$13.00
Suunto M3-D	$19.00

Using the Compass Any compass, no matter how well made, is useless to its owner if he doesn't understand how it works and how to use it. Over the years I've met a disturbing number of hikers, campers, and especially hunters who either don't carry a compass in the woods or don't know how to use the compass they carry.

A good compass is absolutely essential to the woodsman. Human beings do not possess the mysterious sense of direction common to the lower animals. Humans tend to walk in circles in the woods, so it takes just a few square miles to become completely lost. Even if the survivalist isn't sure of his location—after the crash of a light plane, for example—the compass will keep him walking in a straight line toward the nearest highway or other source of rescue.

The first step in learning to use a compass is to understand that it points toward magnetic north all the time. Magnetic north isn't necessarily true north, but since most good maps take into account the amount of "declination" (the discrepancy between true north and magnetic north), this is almost never a problem. The directions shown on a topographical map will be referenced to magnetic north rather than true north. For the purpose of simplification I'll refer to magnetic north simply as "north."

THE COMPASS DIAL

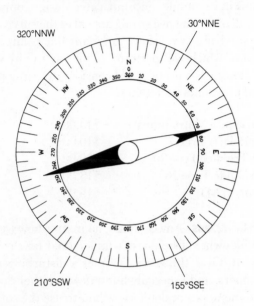

The bezel of the compass is marked in graduations of one degree, beginning at zero—or north—and rotating in a clockwise direction to 360 degrees, which is also zero. Put simply, the points of the compass begin and end at north, which is both the 360- and zero-degree mark.

The compass is also divided into "quadrants," or fourths, with each quadrant equal to ninety degrees. Each of these quadrants represents a direction. The direction found at the ninety-degree mark to the right of north is due east. The direction found at the 180-degree mark (90 + 90 = 180) opposite north is due south.

At 270 degrees (180 + 90 = 270), we find due west. And ninety degrees farther brings us back to 360 degrees, which is also zero or due north. Of course, any return course will be in exactly the opposite direction of the one taken into the woods, or 180 degrees from the original direction. If a hiker enters the forest on a course of 300 degrees west by northwest, the direction that will lead him back out will be 120 degrees east by southeast, or 180 degrees from the original direction (300 − 180 = 120).

Each quadrant is further divided into halves for the purpose of communicating directions. Half of ninety degrees is forty-five degrees. The forty-five degree mark is the dividing line between a direction and its adjacent directions. For instance, the thirty-four degree mark would be stated as "thirty-four degrees north by northeast." Seventy-two degrees would be seventy-two degrees east by northeast. 260 degrees would be 260 degrees west by southwest, and so on.

It's essential that any woodsman entering the woods take a compass reading, or "bearing," before starting his trek to determine the location of roads, railways, and other large landmarks that would be hard to miss. It's difficult to determine which direction leads out when one doesn't know which direction brought him in.

Whenever possible the compass should be complemented by a map. Topographical maps, available from outfitters, Fish and Game field offices, and bookstores are best because they show terrain contours and elevations, which are very handy for avoiding obstacles such as mountains. But any map is better than none.

To plot a course with the map and compass, lay the map on as flat a surface as possible and place the compass on top of it. Align both the map and compass toward north. Determine your present location as closely as possible on the map, and the direction of your objective. Using the map scale of the compass as a straightedge, draw a line (a pencil and pad should be part of any survivalist's navigation kit) connecting the two. Now lay the compass on the map so that the center of the dial is directly on top of the point indicating your present position (this is much easier with a transparent map compass) and read your course direction in degrees at the point where the pencil line interests the bezel. Actual distances can be determined by using the map scale on the compass. This is all the orienteering the person in a survival situation needs to know.

MAGNETIC DECLINATION MAP OF THE UNITED STATES

Add the number of degrees indicated on the map to your compass reading if you are east of the zero declination line.
Subtract if you are west of the zero declination line.

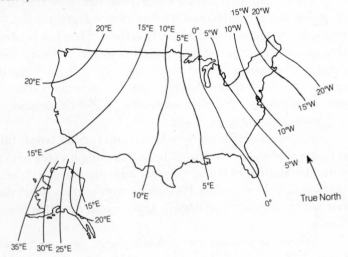

Fire-Starting Tools

Fire is every bit as important to the modern survivalist as it was to Cro-Magnon Man. But unlike our ancient predecessors we have access to fire-making tools and equipment that make the old methods obsolete and unnecessary. Every serious survivalist should become familiar with making and using the bow-and-drill, but it's highly doubtful that any prepared survivalist would ever have to use it to start a fire. Why would a lost hunter or plane-crash survivor expend the energy required to make and use a bow-and-drill when he had a book of (dry) matches in his pocket?

Matches are something every woodsman should have at all times. Used carefully, a single book of matches is capable of starting twenty fires; two books, forty fires. Assuming that the survivalist is walking back to civilization, and that the average person can easily march twenty-five miles a day, if he makes a new campfire each night and doesn't waste any matches, he will have to walk 500 miles before exhausting a single book.

Wooden "strike anywhere" safety matches offer the advantage of being hotter-burning and less apt to be blown out by a breeze, but these can be quite volatile, often igniting against themselves. Many a woodsman, myself included, has had the unpleasant experience of having a pocketful of these little wonders ignite from rubbing against one another. Always carry them in an airtight match holder.

The newest breed of wooden matches is a bit safer. They are equally resistant to being blown out, but will only light when struck against the igniter strip on the side of the box they come in. These can be carried in a match holder, pill bottle, or even wrapped in a plastic sandwich bag as protection against moisture, but they're useless unless a section of the igniter strip is included.

Disposable butane lighters are one of the many miracles of modern technology most of us have come to take for granted. A single Bic, Crickett, or Scripto lighter is the equivalent of about 100 books of matches and has the added advantage of being impervious to water. If it gets dunked all one has to do is wait until the flint and igniter wheel dry out and it's back in business.

But the value of the butane lighter doesn't end when the supply of butane is exhausted. I've found that by removing the metal hood surrounding the gas port the lighter can be used as a spark-thrower to ignite dried grass, cotton fibers, and other fine tinder. It seems the flint in a disposable butane lighter always lasts twice as long as its butane supply, and that can be an advantage in the wilderness.

Chemical fire starters are also a great asset, especially in very cold or wet weather. Military Trioxane bars and the smaller Hexamine tablets, available at most Army-Navy surplus stores, are very stable, have an almost infinite shelf life, and burn with a hot, smokeless blue flame that can be used to start a fire with wet wood or under windy conditions. Either of them can also be used alone to heat water or canned food. Trioxane comes in a box containing three foil-wrapped bars and retails for about two dollars per box. Hexamine tablets come six to a cardboard tube and retail for around one dollar per tube. Both of these are very effective for starting fires under adverse conditions, but I prefer the larger Trioxane bars. Having one of these in my pack has saved my fingers on several subzero mornings when the temperature was so low that I had only seconds in which to get the fire started before my hands turned into frostbitten claws.

The magnesium fire-starting block came onto the market almost a decade ago but has never gained much popularity. This is one of those items that apparently worked fine in the lab but not in the field.

The theory is solid. The unit consists of a palm-sized block of magnesium with a heavy strip of flint embedded in one side. The idea is to use a knife to shave a small pile of magnesium powder from the block, then use the knife to strike a spark from the flint, thereby igniting the flammable powdered magnesium. That's how it's supposed to work, anyway. In reality, the magnesium shavings blow away with the slightest breeze and the knife dulls very quickly, making it progressively harder to shave off more magnesium to replace the shavings that have blown away. The blocks retail for about six dollars at most sporting goods outlets and Army-Navy stores.

Candles are an old tried-and-true fire-starting aid that date back to the early nineteenth century, when sulfur matches were invented. Every woodsman should have at least one "Emergency Candle" in his pocket or kit to help light fires in wet weather. A lighted candle placed under a pile of even the wettest twigs will start a fire, even in a light rain. The real beauty of candles is that they're downright cheap. A package of five retails for around two dollars and can be found in supermarkets, sporting goods, and department stores. Tea candles, which come in their own metal container, are also very inexpensive and in some instances even better.

A magnifying glass can also be used to start fires, but only if the sun is shining. I think we're all familiar with the ability of a magnifying glass to concentrate the rays of the sun into a hot beam that will burn most combustibles, so I won't go into detail about how it works.

The Bow-and-Drill The concept of the bow-and-drill is simple: a wooden drill, or spindle made from dried softwood such as poplar, pine, or basswood, is spun back and forth rapidly against a "fireboard" made from the same material until enough friction and heat are generated to ignite a small pile of dried tinder. That, in a nutshell, is it.

Construction of the bow-and-drill is also simple. The tool has five basic parts: the bow, the bowstring, the handle, the fireboard, and the drill. With a bit of practice the entire tool can be constructed in less than thirty minutes, and a fire started in another twenty to forty minutes. This doesn't even compare to the time it takes to start a fire using some of the modern fire-starting aids, but the bow-and-drill does work and may very well come in handy sometime.

The drill is made from a straight, dry, barkless piece of softwood, usually a section of tree branch. The ideal drill should be approximately twelve inches long, one inch in diameter, and as round and straight as possible to keep wobble during rotation to a minimum. If necessary the drill may be shaved and shaped with a knife. Once a suitable drill has been chosen, the bottom (drill) portion is whittled to a sharp point and the top is rounded as smoothly as possible. Use coarse rock or sandstone to smooth imperfections from the finished drill.

The handle is made from a piece of wood approximately three inches wide by six inches long by two inches thick. If at all possible the handle should be made from a hardwood like oak, cherry, or maple. The edges should be smoothed to fit comfortably in your palm. Using the point of the knife as a drill, dig out and shape a rounded hole that matches the top, rounded portion of the drill. To make the two pieces fit more closely together, rotate the drill by hand in the hole of the handle. The addition of a little sand will help to smooth the rough surfaces in the hole.

The fireboard is made from a piece of softwood about six inches wide by twelve to eighteen inches long and one inch thick, as flat as possible on both sides. It's usually best to make the board by splitting slabs from a section of dead (but not rotten) poplar or pine log with a strong, sharp knife or hatchet until an acceptable board is obtained. Once a board has been selected drill a hole into one corner using the tip of the knife. The hole should be conical, about one-half inch deep and one-half inch wide at the top. The exact location of the hole on the board isn't important, but it should be approximately one-eighth inch from the edge of the board at its widest point. When the hole is finished, a downward-sloping notch is cut into the eighth-inch remaining between its edge and the outside of the board, about one-half inch deep and just slightly narrower than the drill hole.

The bow is made from a green branch of willow, cedar, or any other springy wood. It may also be made from a young sapling. The bow should ideally be about one inch in diameter by 2½ feet in length. Notch crosswise to its length to a depth of one-quarter inch at both ends. Both notches must be on the same side of the bow, which will be outside of the finished bow. If the bow you've selected has a natural curve, use it to your advantage, but be sure the notches are cut into what will be the outside of the bow.

The bowstring can be made from nearly any type of sturdy cord such as a bootlace or length of parachute cord. Tie one end to the bow using a slipknot, making sure that the cord fits securely into the notch at that end. Pull the string until it's taut, but not so tight that it flexes the bow, and tie the free end to the opposite end of the bow, again making certain that it nestles snugly into the notch.

With the bow-and-drill now assembled, hold the bow horizontal to the ground in the right hand (opposite if you're a lefty) and place the drill, rounded end up, between the bow and the string. Wrap the string around the drill one time and place the pointed end of the drill into the hole in the fireboard.

USING THE BOW AND BRILL

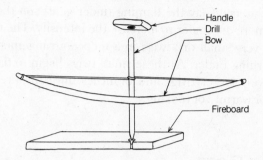

Handle
Drill
Bow

Fireboard

Place the handle on top of the drill with the left hand, making sure that the rounded top of the drill fits loosely but securely into the hole in the handle. Kneel with your right knee resting on the ground and your left foot on the fireboard to help hold it in place. Rest the left elbow on the left knee and press downward firmly but not hard on the handle. With the bow still held horizontal to the ground, begin moving it back and forth with a smooth sawing motion. The drill will spin, first in one direction, then the other, with each stroke. If the drill doesn't spin freely, ease up a bit on the handle. A bit of melted candle wax in the handle hole will help to lubricate it.

As the drill spins against the fireboard it will begin to heat up from friction. A little sand in the fireboard hole will help to increase the friction. Before long the point of the drill will smoke. As you continue to saw the bow back and forth, a charred powder will begin to accumulate in the fireboard notch. As this powder begins to fill the notch and fall upon the pile of dry tinder (crushed dry grass, cotton, dried moss) placed before and under the notch opening, it will begin to glow. At this point your arm will feel tired enough to fall off, but don't quit yet. When enough of this heated wood powder, sometimes called "char," falls upon the tinder it too will begin to smoke.

As soon as the tinder is smoking freely drop the bow and drill and gather the tinder in your cupped palms. Very gently

19

blow into the pile. A prolonged, gentle blow is the best method for coaxing any coal to flames.

At this point lay the flaming tinder gently on the ground and add more dry tinder to increase the intensity. The next step is to pile very small dry twigs in a teepee arrangement on top of the burning tinder. As these small twigs begin to flame, add progressively larger twigs and branches until the fire is large enough for warmth or cooking.

Fishing Gear

There's no reason for anyone venturing into or near the wilderness not to have a good supply of fishing gear. Improvised hooks made of bone or wood and fishing line made of twisted plant fibers are a thing of the past and completely unnecessary for the modern woodsman to survive in the wild. Survivalists have always realized the value of a fishing kit in the forest or swamp where streams are plentiful and fish provide an abundant and reliable source of food every month of the year.

A good working fishing kit is so small and light that it will fit into a jacket pocket. The kit I've used for the past ten years, and the one I provide for each of my own survival students, is self-contained, dirt cheap to make, and unbelievably effective. I've used it to take brook trout, bluegill, perch, rock bass, and I once even caught a five-pound largemouth bass with it.

The kit I use consists of a plastic 35mm film bottle with a snap-on cap. The film bottle is my container of choice for most small items because it's unbreakable, tough, and has a watertight seal. Inside the bottle I place an assortment of long-shank hooks (they seem to be most effective), about a dozen split-shot sinkers, at least thirty feet of twenty-pound-test monofilament line held in a small coil with a rubber band or wire tie, a scented rubber worm, and a Swedish Pimple or spinner for jigging. And even with all this, there's still room for swivels, a steel leader, extra hooks, or a number of other small items.

MAKESHIFT FISHING GEAR

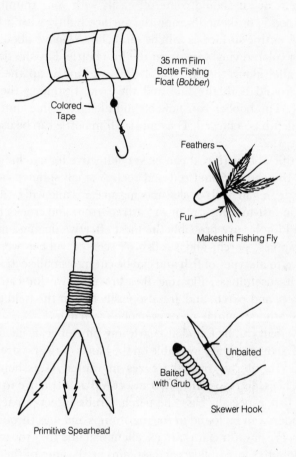

35 mm Film
Bottle Fishing
Float (*Bobber*)

Colored
Tape

Feathers

Fur

Makeshift Fishing Fly

Unbaited

Baited
with Grub

Skewer Hook

Primitive Spearhead

But the film bottle itself is an important part of the fishing kit. With a few wraps of brightly-colored vinyl tape around its circumference it will work efficiently as a fishing float, or "bobber."

As an alternative, making a bobber from a twig is simple. First, select a dry softwood twig about four inches long and three-quarters of an inch in diameter. (These dimensions are not critical and are given only as suggestions.) Remove the bark; if the twig is dry it should come off easily with your thumbnail. If the wood is darkened scrape the surface lightly with a knife until the entire surface is a light tan color. Remove about two inches of colored vinyl tape from the film bottle. Lay the fishing line parallel along the surface of the twig and wrap the tape snugly around both the line and the twig, fastening the two together. The bobber can now be slid along the line until the desired depth is achieved. The emptied film bottle can be used in the same way.

Artificial bait (lures) can be very effective for catching fish without the conventional rod and reel. A small spinner can be used for jigging in pools or slow moving streams and will be active enough in fast-moving streams to attract trout and creek chubs. Swedish Pimples are probably the most effective jigging lure for bass, crappies, perch, and sunfish. A scented rubber worm is attractive to all types of fish and can be cut into small sections to extend its usefulness. Floating flies are effective for catching trout, bass, and perch, and are also easily tied in the field using thread, feathers, animal fur, or even one's own hair.

Live bait can be found at nearly any time of year, including winter. Earthworms are available on the banks of rivers, streams, and lakes until the ground freezes in winter. Grasshoppers, crickets, bees, and most any other insect will be attractive to most types of fish, especially bass and perch. Grubs, insect pupae, and salamanders can be found in rotting stumps and logs throughout the year. Freshwater clams are excellent bait and they too can be found close to shore in lakes and streams at all times of the year. And always bear in mind that fish are cannibalistic creatures. If more live bait is somehow unavailable, the first fish caught can be sacrificed as bait to catch others.

One item that I believe should be a part of any woodsman's kit is the four-tined frog spearhead. A spearshaft can be quickly made from a straight green sapling and fastened securely to the spearhead simply by forcing the tapered shaft into it. The spearhead costs only about three dollars and can be used to take frogs, fish, and even small animals. Rabbit burrows are often shallow and straight, making it simple to thrust the spear through the burrow entrance and impale the occupant. This tactic, like many others in survival, is not pleasant, but when the alternative is starvation the choice is easy.

Shelter Materials

Shelter is a necessity when facing inclement weather conditions. In the north country even a midsummer rain can reduce a person's temperature to the point of hypothermia (a lowering of the internal body temperature). In the winter hypothermia is a very real possibility and adequate shelter is usually necessary just to stay alive.

A poncho is one of the most versatile tools for protection against the elements. It can be worn as a raincoat, wrapped around a sleeping bag or bedroll to keep it dry, used as a waterproof shelter roof, or simply used to cover the survivalist who, for one reason or another, must sleep in the open.

The "space blanket" is another wonder of technology. The basic model is simply a large sheet of reflective aluminum-laminated plastic, usually measuring 7 by 4½ feet. It's reputed to be able to reflect up to 80 percent of a person's body heat back at them. My own experience has been that it doesn't provide sufficient insulation by itself to keep a person warm in cold weather. It does, however, make a wonderful shelter roof, being waterproof and windproof. An added bonus is that its shiny silver coating turns the entire shelter into a giant mirror that is easily spotted from the air. The basic 84×54-inch space blanket, called an Emergency Blanket by some companies, is available for less than three bucks at most department and sporting goods stores. It comes in a compact package and weighs a mere two ounces.

A variation on the basic space blanket is the cloth-backed vinyl "sportsman's" blanket, available in red, silver or woodland camouflage. This blanket has approximately the same dimensions as the space blanket but is a bit more durable and made to

SURVIVAL KNOTS

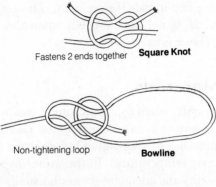

Fastens 2 ends together   **Square Knot**

Non-tightening loop   **Bowline**

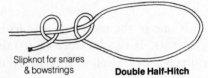

Slipknot for snares
& bowstrings   **Double Half-Hitch**

be used over and over, whereas the basic blanket is designed to be used only once. The sportsman's blanket folds into a compact 8½ × 9½-inch package, weighs twelve ounces, and costs about twelve dollars.

Another inexpensive and effective shelter material is the polypropylene plastic sheeting used as tarpaulins and painters' dropcloths. This material is light, waterproof, windproof, and cheap enough to find a place in everyone's kit. It's available in clear and black, but I recommend the clear because it's more easily spotted from the air and makes a more efficient solar still for collecting and purifying water.

While not absolutely necessary to the construction of an emergency shelter, 100 feet or so of strong, light nylon cord is invaluable for erecting shelters quickly, not to mention the hundreds of other uses it has around camp. Woven nylon parachute cord has a ninety-pound working load and can be found in 100-foot lengths at most Army-Navy surplus stores for about six dollars. Twisted nylon string has a thirty-pound working load and is available in nearly any length imaginable, starting at about three dollars for 200 feet. And, of course, it is always useful to have a good familiarity with some of the basic knots.

Signals

Those in need of rescue should be aware of the techniques for alerting a search party to their whereabouts. The lost or stranded hunter needs to be especially well informed because he hasn't got a lot of time. It's a rather hard fact that most hunters are given up for dead after a maximum of seventy-two hours in cold weather.

The signal flare is a tried-and-true method of signaling, but it can only be effective if the searchers are close enough to see its trail as it arcs through the sky. Even then the flare is visible for only a few seconds and can be obscured from sight by high terrain.

The most common type of signal flare is the single-shot flare pistol. These pistols use a flare cartridge that resembles a twelve-gauge shotgun shell. The gun itself has a break action similar to most single-shot shotguns. But be warned, flare pistols are usually constructed of cast metal or even plastic. *Never* attempt to fire a shotgun shell in one. Flare pistols usually start at around sixty dollars.

Pencil flares are another, more compact type of signal flare launcher. As the name implies, the pencil flare is a compact tube slightly larger than a pencil. Since it's smaller than the flare pistol, it also uses a smaller, less obvious flare. Pencil flares retail for around seventeen dollars for a package of three.

Smoke bombs can be purchased from many Army-Navy and outfitter stores. They're much larger than the novelty smoke bombs sold in department stores and create much more smoke, but like the signal flare their usefulness is limited by range as well as by wind conditions. Smoke bombs sell for about ten dollars apiece.

EMERGENCY GROUND-TO-AIR SIGNALS
THAT CAN BE MADE WITH PIECES OF WEED OR
IN THE SNOW AND SAND

Indicate Direction	This Way	Safe to Land	I Am Okay
K	↑	△	LL

Negative (No)	Affirmative	Not Understood	Need Compass, Map
N	Y	⊥⊥	▢

I Am Injured	Need Medicine	Cannot Proceed	Need Food, Water
I	II	X	F

Loud, piercing whistles have had some value in signaling search parties in the past, particularly in densely forested areas or under foggy conditions. The sound of a whistle will carry for miles in mountainous country. Sport whistles work very well, but there's currently a unit on the market that incorporates a liquid-filled compass, match holder, signal whistle, and lanyard. The entire unit is approximately six inches long by two inches in diameter and composed of orange plastic. It sells for about five dollars and should be a welcome addition to any survival kit.

Flashlights are not only generally useful, they make excellent signaling devices. Technology has made possible flashlights that are brighter and far tougher than anything used by any previous generation of woodsmen. New flashlights, most notably the near-indestructible Mag-Lite, use high-intensity krypton or halogen bulbs that give the standard two-cell D size flashlight as much brilliance as the old six-volt lanterns. Even the AA Mini

Mag-Lite provides more light than standard D-cell flashlights. There are currently several aluminum flashlights on the market but I recommend the Mag-Lite by name because it has a proven track record for durability, bulbs are readily available from most stores, and it's completely American-made. Mini Mag-Lites retail for about twelve dollars (a few dollars more with a belt holster) and around twenty-five dollars for the two-cell D light. Both have adjustable beams that can be focused from broad to spotlight.

As a signal the flashlight is useful only at night, but its beam can be seen from as far as five miles away, depending on the size and power of the light. Considering its utility, it would be foolish for anyone to venture into the wilderness without a good flashlight, spare batteries, and an extra bulb, even if the light is just a cheap plastic model.

Portable radio beacons are a basic part of the emergency gear found on light planes and most larger boats. The radio beacon is a battery-operated transmitter that looks like a walkie-talkie. It doesn't receive signals and can't be used for voice transmission, but it generates a powerful long-range signal tuned to a designated emergency frequency monitored by airports and Coast Guard vessels. The survivor of a plane crash or water emergency can signal rescuers simply by switching the beacon on and leaving it on. This will allow rescue vehicles or aircraft to fix on the position by triangulation.

Fire is also useful as a distress signal, and in some situations it may even be the best way to attract help. A large but controllable signal fire built on the highest point possible will be visible from more than fifteen miles away, depending on weather conditions, and is sure to be seen by passing aircraft. During daylight hours, when a flame is less likely to be seen, the fire can be used as a smoke signal by allowing it to burn down to a hot bed of coals and then partially smothering it with green pine boughs and wet or rotted wood. This will produce a thick cloud of white smoke that's sure to be seen by a firetower or patrolling aircraft.

Hardly anyone knows Morse code these days except a few ham radio operators. Morse code, like the telegraph that used it, has been made obsolete by faster, more efficient methods of communication. But every outdoorsman should know the letters S and O, the components of the emergency SOS signal recognized around the world. SOS is an abbreviation for "Save Our Ship," and was originally intended to be a maritime distress call, but the years have transformed it into a universal call for help. The letter S consists of three dots (. . .), which translates into three shorts signals. The letter O is three dashes (- - -), or three long signals. To send an SOS with a flashlight, for example, the person signaling would flash the beam with three short bursts (S), followed by three bursts of longer duration (O), and finally three more short bursts (S). The SOS signal can also be made with sounds, as with a whistle. In this case the sound would be "Tweet, tweet, tweet. Pause. Tweeeet, tweeeet, tweeeet. Pause. Tweet, tweet tweet."

Survival Firearms

The art of outdoor survival has taken a lot of abuse over the past decade, most of it brought on by paramilitary Rambo-types who try to conceal their true nature by calling themselves survivalists. A true survivalist has no need for full-automatic weapons, oversized ammunition magazines, bayonet studs, folding stocks, or any of the other toys pseudo-survivalists affix to firearms.

But a firearm is an asset to anyone stranded in the wilderness. It isn't nearly as important as the knife, compass, or matches, but it can be very useful as a food gathering tool or signal device. A competent marksman need never go without fresh meat, fowl, or even fish.

The rifle is most often selected as a survival gun for a number of reasons: It has more range, accuracy, and killing power than a handgun or shotgun in any given caliber; it's easier to become proficient with than a handgun; its ammunition is smaller than used in the shotgun; and finally, the rifle is more certain of getting the job done at longer ranges than either of the other two.

Yet even though nearly all experienced outdoorsmen agree that the rifle is best suited for the role of survival gun, there exists some disagreement about which caliber is most capable of meeting the needs of the survivalist. I'm going to go right ahead and say that I believe the .22 Long Rifle is the best choice available for use in an all-around survival rifle.

Why the .22? Versatility is the biggest reason. In the hands of a skilled marksman the vastly underrated Long Rifle cartridge can and has been used to take nearly every edible animal on the North American continent. I've used it successfully to take rabbits, porcupines, squirrels, ruffed grouse, ducks, geese, turkeys, spawning salmon and trout, and even a couple of whitetail deer at distances of up to 100 yards. As a sporting cartridge, the .22 is illegal to use on many of these animals, but the need to eat in a survival situation is recognized by the laws of both the United States and Canada.

Aside from its proven killing power and accuracy, the .22 Long Rifle cartridge is even more attractive because of its small size and portability. The standard box of fifty rounds weighs only six ounces and measures 1 × 1¼ × 2¼ inches. Five hundred rounds are more than sufficient for any contingency—including repeated signaling with gunshots—yet weigh less than four pounds.

A small minority of woodsmen prefer to use the shotgun as a survival gun. They justify their choice by arguing that the shotgun has the same range as the .22 Long Rifle but can knock a goose out of the air or stop a charging grizzly bear with equal effectiveness. The weak point in this argument is that such attacks are rare and can nearly always be avoided by giving potentially dangerous animals a wide berth.

For the woodsman who wants a survival gun but can't decide on a rifle or shotgun, there is a very nice compromise from Savage Firearms. The Model 24 is an over-and-under shotgun/rifle combination and is available in a number of caliber/gauge combinations, like 30-30/20-gauge, .22 Long Rifle/20-gauge, or .22 Long Rifle/.410. When not in use the Model 24 breaks down into three separate pieces—the stock and receiver, the barrels, and the forearm—and fits easily into a full-size backpack.

Following is a list of firearms that I've used and can recommend for use by anyone needing a firearm to provide themselves with food in an emergency. Two of them, the Charter Arms AR-7 and the Marlin 70P, are semi-autos with screw-off barrels that were designed specifically for use as backpack survival rifles. The AR-7 has long been a favorite of canoeists because its receiver and barrel can be detached from and stowed in the hollow plastic stock, making it the world's only floating rifle.

Marlin Model 25 bolt-action .22	$100.00
Charter Arms AR-7 semi-auto .22	$150.00
Savage Model 24 over-and-under	$260.00
Armscor Model 20P semi-auto .22	$90.00
Marlin Model 70P semi-auto .22	$100.00

Marksmanship Far too many sport hunters take to the field with little or no shooting skills, secure in the fact that if they miss they can always go home to a hot meal. But if you're stranded or injured you can't afford to be so blithe concerning your marksmanship. In the wild every single cartridge represents a meal or an important signal.

Like all skills shooting has its own procedures and techniques that must be followed to become even mediocre. First is proper sight alignment. Place the rifle butt against the shoulder with the stock securely nestled into the hollow of the shoulder. Lean forward slightly—never backward. If the gun is equipped with telescopic sights, simply place the intersection of the crosshairs on the target and hold as steady as possible. If the gun has "iron" sights, look through the notch in the rear sight and align the front sight blade with it until the blade sits in the rear sight notch flush with its top. Place the aligned sights directly under the target. Whenever possible, rest the stock forend (not the barrel) on a convenient tree branch or other support to help hold it steady.

RIFLE SIGHTS

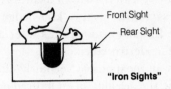

Front Sight
Rear Sight

"Iron Sights"

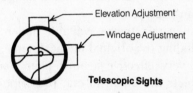

Elevation Adjustment
Windage Adjustment

Telescopic Sights

Next is proper trigger squeeze. More shots are missed because of a jerked trigger than for any other reason. The trigger of any rifle—or pistol for that matter—must always be gently pulled back toward the shooter with the ball of the forefinger, directly opposite the fingernail and ahead of the first joint. The shooter should never know precisely when the gun will fire, but should press the trigger with steadily increasing force while concentrating on keeping the sights aligned with the target. When the firearm discharges it should come as a surprise. The shooter should hold his breath during this exercise to prevent excessive barrel wobble.

That's basically all there is to shooting. Assuming the sights are in proper alignment with the target and the barrel is held steady—and the firing distance is reasonable—the shooter who follows these simple instructions will hit his intended target.

Medical Supplies

Most survival manuals put a great deal of emphasis on herbal medicines, and with good reason. There are literally hundreds of wild plants, trees, and shrubs that have proven medicinal value. The major drawback to herbal medicines is that the woodsman needs to possess a great deal of knowledge to prepare and use them properly. In most instances it's safer and easier to carry a broad supply of modern medicines.

Aspirin is an inexpensive yet fairly effective pain killer. It will help to ease the swelling in an injured or bruised limb, bring down a fever and dampen the pain of minor injuries. Aspirin also works to thin the blood, and so should not be used when internal bleeding is suspected.

Ibuprofen tablets are available under a number of brand names, including the original medical name, Motrin. Ibuprofen tablets are very effective against pain. Four of the over-the-counter tablets are equal to one prescription-strength Motrin tablet. Except for possible stomach upset—always a potential side effect of Motrin—taking four ibuprofen tablets will not harm the user. However, use this dosage only in cases of very severe pain, never exceed it, and don't repeat it more often than once every four hours. Remember, pain is the body's signal that something is wrong. *Never* use a pain-killer to make it possible to walk on an injured leg or to overcome a suspected back injury. Doing so will only make matters worse. It' better to be laid up for a couple of days with a minor injury than for a couple of weeks with an injury compounded by foolishness.

A bar of hand soap should be part of any wilderness first-aid kit. Doctors now agree that the best way to prevent infection in minor cuts and scrapes is not with peroxide, alcohol, mercurochrome, or any of the other popular disinfectants, but simply to wash the wound with soap and water.

Antibiotic ointments such as Neosporin are also necessary to a functional first-aid kit. These ointments take up where the soap and water leave off, providing a protective coating that keeps bacteria out of a wound, as well as antibiotics to kill any germs that might still be there after washing. Most antibiotic ointments also contain zinc oxide to accelerate healing.

Iodine isn't necessary to disinfect cuts, but it's a good idea to include a bottle of it in a medicine kit. It *will* disinfect wounds (although it also destroys skin cells in the process), but it's most important as a water purifier. Two to three drops in a quart canteen will kill any virus, bacteria or trematode (a parasitic organism) living in it. Iodine is also highly poisonous to humans, so never exceed three drops per quart of water and always make certain that some of the disinfected water is sloshed over the mouth of the canteen before drinking from it. Commercially-made iodine water purification tablets are available from most stores that sell camping equipment, but are two to three times more expensive than a bottle of ordinary iodine disinfectant, and tend to disintegrate over time.

Butterfly sutures are a relatively new innovation that have found wide acceptance among outdoorsmen who don't have quick access to medical help but may need to close gaping wounds quickly before serious blood loss can occur. In days past, the only recourse was to stitch the wound closed with a needle and some type of thread. This is not recommended in the less-than-sterile environment of the wilderness because the needle and thread often introduce new infectious organisms that can breed in the closed wound. Nearly as effective as stitches, butterfly sutures are essentially very sticky tapes enclosed in a sterile envelope. After thoroughly washing the wound and stopping the bleeding as much as possible, the butterfly suture is used to pull the wound closed and hold it there.

Safety tape is another relatively new item that was originally designed to wrap the fingers of factory workers to prevent minor cuts and scratches. The tape is made by applying a latex coating over surgical-grade cotton gauze and wrapping it in roll form. It will stick tenaciously to itself but will not adhere to anything else, including skin. Since most cuts sustained by woodsmen are on the fingers, safety tape is perfect for bandaging even serious wounds on the digits quickly and with almost no blood loss. After washing the wound thoroughly, apply a generous coating of antibiotic ointment and wrap the finger with several snug (not tight) layers of safety tape. This will close the wound. Leave the tape on for at least twelve hours before carefully removing it to apply a looser wrap over a fresh coating of antibiotic ointment. Safety tape is also useful for wrapping sprained joints and applying splints to broken bones. It comes in a variety of widths up to three inches and an assortment of colors, although only white should be used as a bandage.

At the time of this writing there is only one source for safety tape that I'm aware of. The company is General Bandages, Inc., Box 909, Morton Grove, Illinois 60053. A free roll is available from them for the asking.

Multivitamin tablets are an often overlooked component of the well-equipped medical kit. It seems ironic that so many of the folks who religiously take vitamins at home will forget about them in the woods. In a survival situation a good multivitamin can help to stave off the effects of malnutrition by providing the vitamins and minerals necessary to remain healthy and energetic.

The toothbrush is another vital accessory that many woodsmen, even trained survivalists, tend to forget. A gum infection can set in quickly in the woods and can become an abcess without proper dental hygiene. A tooth abcess can literally kill its victim overnight with a fever that can easily top the 100-degree mark. Toothpaste is optional, but no woodsman should ever be without a toothbrush.

In a pinch the twig brush, an old-fashioned type of tooth cleaner that preceded the modern toothbrush, will suffice. The twig brush is made by chewing a section of green twig (I recommend the witch hazel shrub) until the end is frayed and fibrous. The frayed end is then used to scrub the teeth and gums. Care should be taken to avoid using twigs from poisonous shrubs like Dogwood. Maple, oak, poplar, birch, beech, and even pine can be safely used to make a twig brush.

For those going into very remote places like the Canadian outback or the Alaskan frontier, prescription drugs can be a real asset. Penicillin, xylocaine, and light-prescription pain killers can sometimes be obtained by scheduling an appointment with the family doctor and explaining that the drugs may be necessary because medical facilities will be beyond reach during the excursion. Any doctor worth his salt will question your motives at length before consenting to write a prescription, and will probably have a good bit of advice to offer concerning the use of prescription drugs in the wilderness. Listen carefully to this advice and take notes; it may save your life in an emergency. Most doctors will also ask that you return any unused drugs when you come back.

A well-stocked emergency medical kit can be invaluable in a survival situation, and may even save a life. It need not be large or heavy, but it must be as functional and efficient as possible. Adequate medical kits can be made from small duffles, lunch boxes or even a zip-lock plastic bag. My own medical kit consists of several ordinary hinged bar-soap containers filled with an assortment of small items and held closed by heavy rubber bands. The entire kit is stored in a heavy zip-lock bag and stowed in my backpack. I prefer to make my own medical kit because premade kits always seem to lack several of the items I consider necessary. Following is a list of recommended items for an emergency medical kit:

1 tube antibiotic ointment
1 roll 1" wide safety tape
Butterfly sutures, assorted sizes
1 bottle ibuprofen tablets
1 bottle aspirin
1 bottle iodine
1 small bar hand soap
1 toothbrush
1 pair tweezers
1 small pair scissors
6 alcohol prep pads
1 pair toenail clippers

1 section latex rubber tubing, 2' long (for tourniquets)
1 package glucose tablets (sugar)
1 bottle multivitamins
1 roll cotton gauze
1 package sewing needles, assorted sizes
1 styptic pencil

Miscellaneous Items

Only size and weight limit the utility of any survival kit. It stands to reason that the size and complexity of a deer hunter's survival kit will be less than that of a boater or off-road driver. The aforementioned items are those that have proven useful many times and all of them are recommended for inclusion in any survivalist's kit. The following items are also very useful, but probably none of them are critical to survival. Of course, whether a particular item is necessary or not depends on the season, terrain, individual wants, and a host of other factors.

Most of us had slingshots as children. Those of us who are older than we care to admit probably made our own slingshots from rubber inner tubes and a Y-shaped stick. They were effective, but not nearly as powerful as the latest generation of high-velocity slingshots powered by tough latex rubber tubing. Using marbles or ball bearings as ammunition, this new breed of slingshot is easily capable of taking most small game animals, providing that the shooter has enough skill to hit them. Some models even fold into a compact unit for easy storage in a backpack.

Spare socks are very important in cold weather. Wet socks do little to keep the feet warm, and wearing wet socks in cold weather can result in trenchfoot, frozen toes, even gangrene. The military has long realized the importance of clean, dry socks in cold weather, especially under conditions of prolonged exposure.

Leather gloves are an important item to any woodsman in any weather. During warm weather a pair of heavy leather gloves will protect the hands from scratches, cuts, blisters, and burns.

In cold weather—with a pair of wool liners inside—they will like-wise protect them from frostbite and cold. GI-issue gloves are adequate for all-around use but the leather used to make them isn't as heavy as that used in some of the civilian models, most notably those from the Wells-Lamont company. Ironically, the less durable military gloves often sell at twice the price of civilian work gloves.

The wide-brimmed military-type bush hat is more versatile than many folks realize. It offers nothing in the way of warmth during cold weather, but when it's warm the bush hat will help to keep the sun off the wearer's head and out of his eyes. Being made of heavy cloth it can be saturated with water and worn wet to keep the head cool, yet still retain enough water repellency to keep a pouring rain out of your eyes. I've used my own bush hat to filter the mud, silt, and microscopic organisms from swamp water, as a berry bucket, as a potholder for campfire cooking, and even as a trap to catch minnows for use as bait. For the hunter, the rumpled, misshapen apearance of the bush hat works to make the distinctly out-of-place shape of the human head less recognizable in almost any terrain.

The "Dog Rag" is nothing more than a very large handker-chief or square of heavy cloth. It can be used to filter muddy water, as an emergency tourniquet, as a potholder, tied at the four corners to make a hobo bindle, as a sweatband, or a wash-cloth. In desert areas the dog rag can also be used to sponge up the dewdrops that collect on rocks in the early morning hours. The gathered dew can then be wrung out into a canteen cup, tin can or directly into the mouth.

Large, colored wire ties, like those included with some brands of plastic garbage bags, are infinitely useful in the wild. They can be used to quickly fasten together the frame of an emergency shelter or bundle dried grasses into an insulated sleeping mat. They can be used, one per pair of eyelets, to replace a bootlace that has been sacrificed to make a snare or hunting bow. They will even serve to fasten branches, ferns, and leafy boughs to one's clothing as hunting camouflage.

The electronics of today are so compact and energy efficient that there's no reason whatsoever not to have a radio receiver on any venture away from civilization. Personal AM/FM receivers are smaller than a deck of cards and can operate on two AAA alkaline cells for a week or more. My own "backpack radio" is an electronic wonder that receives AM, FM, VHF-TV, and Weather Band frequencies. It cost less than seventeen dollars and will operate on four AA batteries for a month when used for about three hours each day. A good radio receiver can be important for maintaining the morale of a stranded woodsman by constantly reminding him that civilization still exists. The receiver is also valuable for the weather reports it provides, especially if it has Weather Band capability.

A sewing kit can be valuable not only to the survivalist but also to the recreational woodsman who is neither lost nor stranded. Clothing tears, ripped backpack seams, and a variety of other frequent damage that can be repaired only be needle and thread are common to wilderness travel. A very workable sewing kit can be made by placing a small spool of thread and a package of assorted sewing needles in a 35mm film bottle. The total cost of this type of sewing kit is less than seventy-five cents.

Even though this section deals with miscellaneous, non-critical tools of survival, I very much recommend that any woodsman have with him a GI-type plastic canteen, canteen cup, canteen cover, and nylon pistol belt. The canteen will of course carry water, the canteen cup makes an excellent emergency mess kit, the canvas cover will help to keep the water in the canteen cool—if it has been soaked through at the time the canteen is filled—and the heavy, grommeted pistol belt is a handy place to carry a survival knife, medical kit, pouches, and nearly all the smaller components of a practical survival kit. My own survival kit consists of a U.S. Army LBE (Load Bearing Equipment) harness, which is basically just a pistol belt with heavy canvas suspenders attached. This outfit has little use in and of itself, but it provides the most efficient and comfortable method of carrying other survival equipment that I've ever found. I have a razor-sharp USAF

Survival Knife taped securely to the right shoulder strap (I'm left-handed) in the upside-down position for quick and easy access. The two ammo pouches attached to the belt contain fishing tackle, matches, sewing kit, medical gear, Trioxane bars, .22 ammunition, and an assortment of other items too numerous to list. Also attached to the belt is a small map pouch that contains a Silva map compass, a stainless steel mirror, and a laminated, waterproof map of the area I intend to be traveling. Occasionally I carry two canteens and still have pleny of room to attach extra pouches, a machete or hatchet, and just about anything else that can be feasibly attached to the belt or suspenders. This LBE outfit is a completely self-contained survival kit that wears comfortably and weighs less than fifteen pounds with two full canteens.

The importance of a good insect repellent depends on the terrain and the weather. In the snow or desert it has little value, but if you're traveling through or near a swampy area in warm weather, an effective insect repellent can be worth as much as any piece of gear in your kit. Mosquitoes are usually the least of a swamp-tromper's worries; more important are the 300 species of horsefly and deerfly (family Tabanidae) and the 600 species of blackfly (family Simuliidae). These parasitic flies are all very determined biters and all potentially dangerous to humans. Deerflies and horseflies both inflict bites that are quite painful, often bleed freely, and swell into large wheals that can itch intensely for several days. These two flies are credited with the ability remove up to a pint and a half of blood from a domestic animal in a single day. A human without protection in areas of heavy infestation could be in real danger.

**DEERFLY
(FAMILY TABANIDAE)**

Blackflies also pose a danger to the unprepared. Their bite is painless but always bleeds freely, and is followed by a dime-size wheal that itches intensely for

**BLACKFLY
(FAMILY SIMULIIDAE)**

several days. This fly has been known to kill thousands of animals in a single season and humans exposed to areas of heavy blackfly infestation have in many cases required hospitalization.

All three of these flies have a proven ability to transmit a variety of sometimes fatal diseases, including tularemia. Less noticeable ticks and chiggers also transmit a variety of diseases, most notably Lyme disease.

There are a number of wild plants that can be used as an effective insect repellent (especially catnip and other mints), but few are as effective or as convenient as a single bottle of repellent containing DEET stashed in the survival kit. I do not recommend carrying an aerosol spray because the propellants used in most of them are harmful to the ozone layer, and they take up too much room in the kit. A small bottle of Muskol brand repellent contains 100% DEET and will last for weeks in the wild.

In the absence of insect repellent, the survivalist can protect himself by covering his face, hands, and other exposed areas with a layer of mud. Clothing should be buttoned as snugly as possible around the wrists and neck, and trouser legs should be bloused or tied securely around the ankles. Small, smoky "smudge" fires can be set around the perimeter of the camp to deter mosquitoes after dark and help the survivalist get a good night's sleep. Smudge fires are made by building a small, hot fire and then partially smothering it with wet leaves, grass or pine needles. With a good bed of coals, a smudge fire will smolder for several hours and produce enough smoke to repel biting insects.

BLOODROOT
(SAGUINARIA CANADENSIS)

Blooms late spring to fall. White flower in front of single blue-green leaf. Grows up to 10 inches tall. Red sap from root and stem can be applied to skin as an insect repellant.

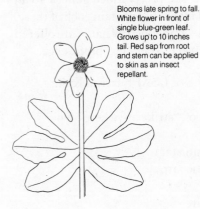

Mint Family. Blooms from early summer to early fall in moist, rich soil. Flower heads clustered, ranging from white to pale violet. Leaves contain an oil toxic to insects.

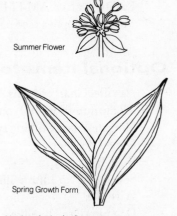

CATNIP
(NEPETA CATARIA)

COMMON TANSY
(TANECETUM VULGARE)

WILD LEEK
(ALLIUM TRICOCCUM)

Summer Flower

Spring Growth Form

Blooms in late summer with clusters of small yellow ray flowers. Plant may be more than 5 feet tall, but 2 feet is normal. Juice of entire plant repels all insects. Toxic if eaten.

Member of onion family. Strong-smelling edible bulb. Flowers white to pink. Juice of entire plant repels insects.

Recommended Items for the Survival Kit

No survival kit will provide for every contingency in every environment, but the following items are pretty much generic to all conditions. Any working survival kit should contain each of these, although those that have been recommended by name are offered merely as suggestions and are subject to personal preference.

Survival Knife, Schrade M7-S or USAF Survival Knife
Compass, Silva Type 3
Matches, wooden, waterproof, "strike anywhere" type
Butane lighter
Fishing kit (in 35mm film canister)
Space blanket or large plastic tarp
Nylon cord, 100 feet
Flashlight, AA Mini Mag-Lite
Signal flares, gun or pencil type, with launcher
Fire-starting tablets, Trioxane or Hexamine
Candle
Canteen, with metal cup, cover and belt
Spare socks, 1 pair, wool
Radio receiver, AM-FM with Weather Band
Medical supplies (see page 31)

Optional Items for the Survival Kit

.22 rifle, Charter Arms AR-7 or Marlin 70-P
.22 ammunition, 100 rounds, Remington Viper
Slingshot, latex tubing type
Gloves, leather
Bush hat
Sewing kit (in 35mm film canister)
Wire ties
Dog rag (large handkerchief)
Insect repellent, bottle, 100% DEET
Spearhead, frog, 3-tined
Prescription drugs (xylocaine, penicillin)

What Do I Do First?

It's safe to say that anyone who suddenly finds himself thrust into a do-or-die survival situation will not be in a clear state of mind. This will be particularly true if he's been injured.

Panic is the mortal enemy of anyone in a survival situation. It can and does cause people to do things that are counter-productive to their survival, even to the point of being suicidal. In primitive man the adrenalin charge of panic was an instinctive survival reaction that gave him the strength to outrun or fight free of immediate danger, but modern man has the ability to plan his way out of a precarious state of affairs. The same capacity for logic and ingenuity that allowed *Homo sapiens* to become master of his environment also gives him an unsurpassed aptitude for survival, an ability to think abstractly, effectively utilize the materials at hand, and adapt to almost any set of conditions.

Since panic is a non-cerebral function, it can be most effectively controlled by maintaining a logical approach to the task of staying alive. The first thing the survivalist must do is make himself as comfortable as possible. The critical thinking portion of the mind is seriously hampered by physical discomfort, so the survivalist needs to address the requirements of his body before attempting to devise an escape plan. He should apply first aid to any injuries, take an analgesic if in pain, build a fire to warm himself and find or construct a shelter if the weather is inclement.

Once he has established a base camp and made himself as comfortable as possible, the survivalist can then take stock of both his supplies and his situation. Assuming that he has with him a well-equipped survival kit and that each of its components has withstood the ordeal up to that point, he can use map and compass to determine his approximate location, learn what obstacles lie between himself and civilization, and plot the most direct route back home. If he has a working radio receiver, he should use it, not only to gather weather reports and forecasts, but also as entertainment.

Proper attitude is also a vital part of the survival process. The way one perceives his situation is at least as important as his knowledge and skill. A successful survivalist is never lost, only momentarily perplexed. He may wonder when he'll get home, but never if he'll get home. The woodsman who sees a sudden snowstorm as beautiful and natural has a far greater chance of staying alive than one who regards it as cold and dismal. If chickadees, squirrels and deer mice are able to sustain life through the worst conditions nature can offer, how can the well-prepared survivalist have any doubt in his own ability to do the same?

In most cases, the survivalist's best option will be to walk back to civilization. Before starting the trek, make certain that you have as good an idea of where you're headed as possible. Travel as lightly as you can, but not to the point of leaving behind transportable tools that might have critical importance on the trail. If packaged food is available, it should make up most of the weight carried because the pack will become lighter as the food is consumed. And remember, there is absolutely nothing to prevent you from taking as many rest periods as you feel are necessary. At least one pseudo-survival school includes a military-style "forced march" as part of its curriculum, a ridiculous exercise that has no application in real life and is in fact counterproductive to survival. Never push yourself to the point of exhaustion because a tired mind and body are apt to make dangerous mistakes. Based on my own experiences, a cold, tired survivalist who continues to push on after his body tells him to stop will become irritable and jumpy and may go right over the edge into a blind panic.

In a nutshell, the secret to survival is to be kind to yourself. If you're cold, build a fire; if you're hungry, eat; and if you're tired, rest. Believe in yourself and never doubt your own capabilities. All of us are born with an inherently powerful survival instinct. That, a few basic pieces of equipment, and a little bit of knowledge are all that will be required to emerge alive and healthy from the most challenging wilderness survival situation. Believe it.

SURVIVAL SHELTERS

Beavers build lodges, deer head for the thick swamp, and coyotes excavate dens in the earth. Unlike humans, all wild animals have natural protections against the ravages of weather and a lifetime in which to become acclimated to life in the out-of-doors. If these creatures have need for shelter, then it stands to reason that our own need to escape the weather is many times greater. In the northern United States and all of Canada hypothermia is a potential danger every month of the year. Even in July a sudden thunderstorm can bring with it sleet, hail, or even snow and the temperature can drop as much as forty degrees Fahrenheit in the space of a couple of hours.

Basic Shelter Requirements

Survival shelters are relatively easy to build if one has just a little knowledge of their construction. All of them are made from the usually abundant materials at hand. Dead branches and saplings are employed to make the frames, shorter sticks and branches form the roof latticework, and wet leaves, snow, ferns, or just plain dirt can be used to seal out the elements. As with all other aspects of survival, imagination and ingenuity are the keys to success.

Cold weather is undoubtedly the most common life-threatening condition anyone in a survival situation will face. Wind and freezing temperatures have caused the deaths of more woodsmen than all other factors combined, primarily because the average outdoor recreationalist is unprepared to weather a winter storm. Nearly all cold weather fatalities occur among sport hunters, a group for whom taking to the wilderness without proper clothing, preparation, or training is almost traditional. In a study conducted by the NRA in 1978 it was determined that the person least likely to survive an extended stay in the wilderness was the armed sport hunter.

Wet, rainy weather can be every bit as dangerous as freezing weather, even though temperatures may be well above freezing. A cold downpour on a sixty-degree day will literally wash away its victim's body heat, leaving him wet, cold, and ill prepared for the sudden drop in temperature that's sure to come after the sun sets. Most experienced woodsmen agree that the best clothing for retaining body heat in wet weather is made from wool. Gore-Tex will help to keep you dry, Thinsulate will keep you warm when you're dry, but only wool will keep you warm when you're soaking wet.

Snow in and of itself is probably the least threatening weather condition. In fact, a 20-degree day with snow on the ground will seem noticeably warmer than the same day without snow. The same insulating qualities that make a snow-filled forest so quiet will also make it feel warmer. Snow can actually be used to protect oneself against the dangers of cold weather because it's abundant, easy to work with, and entirely effective for manufacturing windproof walls and roofs. The most serious danger from the snow is its brightness, which can cause a debilitating —if temporary—affliction known as "snow blindness," especially in bright sunlight. Snow blindness should always be guarded against by wearing sunglasses or a brimmed hat to shade the eyes. If neither of these is available, fashion emergency goggles by tying around your head a broad strip of birch bark with narrow eye slits cut into it.

On the reverse end of the spectrum, the sun can be as dangerous as any other weather condition. Prolonged exposure to a hot sun can cause dehydration, heat exhaustion, and finally, heat stroke. Just as hot is the opposite of cold, so too are the requirements of a hot weather shelter the opposite of the cold weather shelter. Where the cold weather shelter needs dead air to retain the user's body heat, the hot weather shelter needs to breathe and have as much air circulation as possible. An effective hot weather shelter can be made simply by erecting a sloped, lightproof roof over a frame, leaving the sides, front and back open to allow any air currents to pass unobstructed. The space blanket works very well here. The roof should face south to keep out as much sun as possible, and traveling through open country should be restricted to the hours between dusk and dawn. The shade provided by the roof will be approximately ten degrees cooler than the outside temperature and should be comfortable enough to allow the survivalist to sleep through the heat of the day. Perspiration wastes water; by traveling only at night in hot, open terrain, precious water will be conserved and the potential for heat exhaustion reduced.

A thick, insulating bed is absolutely vital in cold weather and is even a good idea on a summer night. The earth is the world's best heat sink and it will absorb a human's body heat faster than it can be generated, resulting in a case of hypothermia that can range from mild to life threatening.

Beds need not be fancy or difficult to make. My own favorite winter bed is made from lengths of dead poplar or cottonwood logs. When these short-lived softwoods die the tops break off in the wind, leaving sections of trunk sticking above the winter hard-pack. These dead trunks are easy to break off and several of them laid side by side on the snow with a thick covering of pine boughs will provide as much insulation from the ground as possible. Building a fire on a similar platform next to the bed will allow you to keep warm while sleeping outside in clear weather. If one is traveling and can avoid building a shelter at the end of a day's trek, why waste the effort?

Fire is one of the survivalist's best friends. It allows him to cook his food, light the darkness, and, most important, keep warm. But there's more to keeping warm than just lighting a fire. You need to harness as much heat from the flames as possible. Sitting in front of a blazing fire in subzero weather will keep only the front of the body warm. To be as effective a heater as possible the warmth of the flames needs to be focused through the use of a reflector, either a natural feature or one erected by the survivalist himself. A rock cliff or dirt bank makes an excellent reflector, as does a space blanket suspended vertically on two poles. Place your body between the reflector and the fire. Direct heat from the flames will warm the portion of your body facing the fire while reflected heat from behind will warm the other side. (The principle is the same as that used in a convection oven.) For maximum heat reflection, place reflectors on three or four sides of the fire. Additional reflectors can be constructed from a dense latticework of branches stood on end to form a wall and stationed a minimum of four feet from the flames.

A fire used to heat a shelter should be positioned directly in front of the shelter entrance, about four feet away, and surrounded on three sides by reflectors. The reflectors will impede the circulation of cold outside air and focus the heat from the fire directly on the door of the shelter. With this configuration, the stranded woodsman on a thick insulating bed inside the shelter will be comfortable even in a subzero blizzard.

The Lean-To

The lean-to is undoubtedly the most familiar outdoor shelter. It's the shelter most often used by movie survivalists and the one most often taught to students in outdoor survival schools. The lean-to is simple and quick to build, uses materials found in almost every type of terrain, and like any good emergency shelter, it can be constructed without tools.

The frame of the lean-to is a simple design. It consists of a main crosspiece held horizontal and about four feet off the ground by a pole or even a live tree at either end. The crosspiece will have to be strong enough to support the roof, so it should be made from a stout, heavy sapling four to six inches in diameter. The ends of the crosspiece are fastened securely to the vertical uprights by notching the uprights and tying the crosspiece in place with cord, or by simply using an existing branch or Y to support the crosspiece.

The fastened crosspiece should be capable of supporting the survivalist's entire body weight without coming loose at either end. Accumulated snow can add more than a hundred pounds of weight to the roof and a windstorm can break large dead branches loose from overhead. Having the roof fall in or a large branch come crashing through can completely ruin a good night's sleep.

With the crosspiece in place, the rest is simple and quick. Lay as many stout saplings as possible at a sloping angle across the crosspiece. These saplings need not be green, but must not be rotten, because they too may be required to support considerable weight. Candidates should be a

THE LEAN-TO

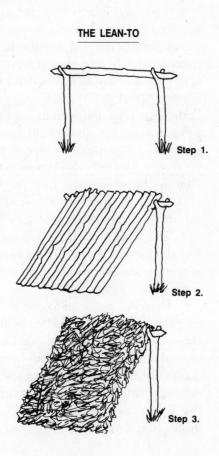

Step 1.

Step 2.

Step 3.

49

minimum of two inches in diameter and at least seven feet long. The ends that rest on the ground should be kept as even with one another as possible, regardless of how far the opposite ends stick out beyond the crosspiece. In fact, those saplings that do stick out from the crosspiece will provide a convenient place to hang wet clothing, firearms, and other assorted gear.

When all the roof poles are in place over the crosspiece, the shelter will be strong but not waterproof or windproof. The easiest and fastest method of weatherproofing the roof is to cover it with a space blanket, poncho, or large piece of polyurethane plastic held down and in place by the addition of several more poles, sticks, and branches.

In winter the roof can also be finished by adding a layer of packed snow. In a hardwood forest there is always a thick layer of flattened, decaying leaves that can be peeled from the ground in sections and placed like shingles over the roof poles, beginning at the lowest end and overlapping them as you go up so that water will run down the slope of the roof without leaking inside. The industrious woodsman who plans on staying in the same place for several days may also choose to fill the gaps with a mixture of mud and dried grasses. In a pinch the old Boy Scout method of shingling the roof with a layer of leafy branches or pine boughs will also work, but this is the least effective technique.

The protective qualities of the lean-to are minimal at best. The sloping roof is an excellent heat reflector, but the open sides allow free circulation of cold air and will admit windblown rain or snow.

However, the lean-to can be modified and turned into an excellent cold-weather shelter by adding another sloping roof on the open side of the crosspiece. Doing so will give the shelter a peaked roof, cut the flow of air by more than half, and effectively double the amount of sleeping and storage area under the roof. Adding yet another wall to cover the open back side, and placing a fire at the opening, will turn the modified lean-to into a well-insulated and easy-to-heat cold-weather shelter.

The Debris Hut

The debris hut, also known as a rubbish hut, is one of the best emergency cold-weather shelters. The snow dugout is just as good, but it requires three to four feet of hardpack snow to build and is meant for use in late winter in snow country. The debris hut can be built quickly in areas where there is little or no snow because its construction uses branches, leaves, and other natural forest debris, although a layer of packed snow can be added to completely seal the outside.

The frame of the debris hut begins with a single stout pole eight to ten feet long. One end of the pole is supported in the crotch of a heavy branch where it joins the tree trunk or it may be lashed in place by notching the trunk and tying it securely with cord. The elevated end of the main support should be no less than four feet above the ground. Again, the main support should be strong enough to support the builder's weight after being fastened in place.

The next step is to begin laying thick branches across the main support from either side, beginning at the highest point and working toward the ground. These branches are both part of the frame and the roof. They simply lay across the main support at an angle and are held in place by the other branches and their own weight. Seen from the end, they form an inverted V shape that gets increasingly smaller as the roof follows the main support down to the ground.

The entrance to the debris hut can be made by simply leaving it open at the high end, but I prefer to seal the end and fashion a doorway, also shaped like an inverted V, in the high side next to the supporting tree trunk. The doorway to this and any other cold-weather shelter should always be kept as small as possible to prevent outside air from circulating through it—it should always face downwind.

When the roof frame is completed, fill the gaps by packing them with wet leaves, moss, ferns, or mud and grass. A space

DEBRIS HUT

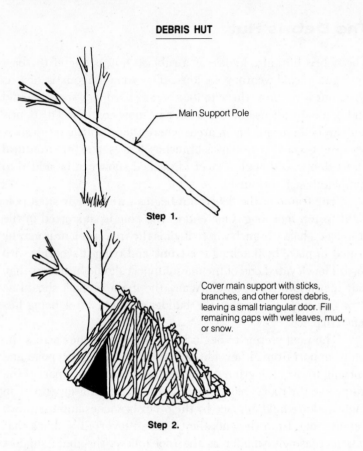

Main Support Pole

Step 1.

Cover main support with sticks, branches, and other forest debris, leaving a small triangular door. Fill remaining gaps with wet leaves, mud, or snow.

Step 2.

blanket can also be draped over the frame and held in place by heavy sticks, to form a waterproof and highly reflective roof covering that can be spotted easily by a passing aircraft. If snow is available, I recommend finishing off the exterior of the shelter with a packed layer several inches thick.

The finished shelter should be just large enough to comfortably contain the woodsman's body after covering the floor inside with heavy branches and a thick layer of pine boughs, leaves, ferns, or any other dry and airy insulating material. This shelter is heated primarily by the sleeper's own body heat, although a fire placed at the entrance and surrounded by reflectors will help considerably.

In foul weather—namely subzero winter blizzards—I recommend foregoing a fire altogether and sealing the entrance with a thick mat of woven branches. Sealed thus, the debris hut is impervious to even the worst weather and retains the sleeper's body heat like a cocoon. There will be very little air circulation through the woven door (just enough to breathe), and that means that nearly all of the heat generated inside will remain inside to keep the occupant warm.

The debris hut can be built from start to finish in well under three hours, and provides more protection from the elements than a tent or most other emergency shelters. I can personally vouch for its lifesaving capability. Even without a fire, the sealed debris hut will keep a lost or stranded woodsman alive through several days of arctic weather with wind chill factors under fifty degrees below zero Fahrenheit.

The Shingle Hut

The origin of this shelter lies in the culture of the Chinook Indians who inhabited the coasts of what are now Oregon, Washington, and British Columbia. The Chinooks built their homes using thick planks split from pine logs and pegged into place. Most other tribes were nomadic, moving from place to place with the change in seasons, but Chinook villages were permanent and their lodges, which were actually more like modern-day houses, reflected their stability.

The shingle hut begins with a large, sturdy frame that usually resembles that used for the double-sided lean-to, although I've also built shingle huts on the smaller debris-hut frame. Once the frame is securely assembled the shingled roof is added.

The shingles are made from the rotting stumps of dead, fallen trees and their trunks. The soft inner core of a dead tree is always the first part to rot away, leaving a solid outer shell. These hollow stumps and logs are plentiful in almost every forest or swamp and are easy to break into slabs that can be used as shingles. A firm pull or kick against the side of a hollow stump will break off a large section of slightly curved wood. A couple dozen of these will be sufficient to cover the roof of a small one-man survival shelter. Large slabs of loose outer bark also make good shingle material.

When placing the shingles always begin nearest the ground and work upward, overlapping the last shingle with the next. This arrangement will help to make the roof watertight in a heavy rain and keep out as much wind as possible.

The shingle hut is basically a fair-weather shelter, although snow can be used to completely seal it against the elements. The shelter itself is sturdy and will probably stand for years, making it a good choice for someone who may be stranded for an extended period in mild weather. Construction time is a bit longer than three hours in most cases, depending on the availability of shingle material.

The Dugout

This shelter is based on front-line military bunkers used in wartime. A well-constructed dugout is as solid and permanent as any house, and is the best choice for a stranded woodsman who may have to wait an indefinite period of time due to weather or personal injury. A survivalist stranded in the Canadian outback at the onset of winter might opt to await rescue rather than take the chance of being caught in a hard blizzard while attempting to walk out, especially if the terrain he's in is favorable to survival.

The one drawback of the dugout is that it requires a large cavity to be excavated in the side of a low hill. If the survivalist (we'll assume he's a plane-crash survivor) has a folding entrenching tool, the job can be accomplished with ease. If he doesn't have an entrenching tool or shovel, the dugout can still be excavated with a slab of wood and bare hands, but it will take the better part of a day to do it and burn a couple thousand calories. These are things that need to be considered before deciding to build the

EARTH DUGOUT

Long-Term Extreme Cold Weather Shelter
(Shown in Cross Section)

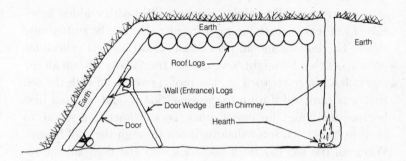

dugout. The type of shelter used depends on food supply, skill, equipment, and the expected duration of a stay in the wild.

But if all options have been considered and the answer still comes up dugout, work should begin immediately. The first step is to select a location. Low hills are my first choice, as long as they're located on high ground where rain runoff or melting spring snow won't flood the shelter. The peaks of larger hills are also good candidates for a dugout, but if the hill is very high the survivalist will burn valuable calories climbing back up it every time he returns to the shelter. Still, locating the shelter on a tall, bald hill might be the best decision in some cases because a signal fire, flare, or reflective space blanket will be more visible to passing aircraft.

Once a site has been selected the real work begins. Those without a shovel or entrenching tool will need a large, sturdy slab of wood to dig away the soil after loosening it and a knife to cut through the ever-present tree roots. It will be slow, hard work. The finished excavation may be as large as the builder wishes, but four feet deep by seven feet long by seven feet wide is large enough to spend a comfortable winter in. Keep all excavated soil in a pile nearby because it will be used later to cover the roof.

When the excavation is finished it should look like a square hole cut into the side of a hill, with the top side open. Make the roof by laying several large, dead logs across the hole with as little gap between each one as possible until they cover the entire top of the excavation. Remaining gaps are filled with wadded handfuls of wet leaves, ferns, or anything else that can be stuffed into them. The builder should periodically crawl inside to check for open spots that he might have missed from above. When all the cracks have been stopped up, the roof is re-covered with the soil that was removed during excavation. Sod should be used first because its dense clusters of grass roots will act as a screen to prevent looser soil from shaking down through the roof beams. When all the sod has been laid back over the log roof, the remainder of the soil is simply piled on top of it. The finished roof will be thick, well insulated and waterproof in even the fiercest rainstorm.

But the front side of the dugout is still open and must be covered. When one is facing the possibility of a winter with temperatures that are likely to plummet to twenty below or worse, without a wind chill factor, making the shelter as warm and functional as possible is literally a matter of life and death. It must be as enclosed and well insulated as possible.

The best way I've found to cover the front of the dugout shelter is to lean more logs and large branches against the outside at a vertical angle, placing them side by side with as little gap between each one as possible. This will form a sloping wall that will provide a bit more room inside, while the incline provides a runoff for rain.

The center of the front wall must be left open to form the doorway, which should be kept as small as possible. When the walls on either side of the doorway are finished and the entrance is the desired size, plug the gaps between logs and cover them as thoroughly as possible with dirt. Again, sod should be placed over the logs first and loose soil piled on top of that.

The door itself is a separate unit that opens from the inside. A door that opens outward is always a bad idea in snow country, where a typical snowstorm may dump up to three feet of heavy, wet snow in less than twenty-four hours, making it impossible to open the door.

The survivalist who is well prepared with a good supply of parachute cord or heavy nylon string can make his door by lashing a row of large, straight branches to a horizontal crosspiece at either end. If cordage is unavailable, the door can be constructed by weaving a heavy mat of green branches together, but this type of door is far less effective than the former and considerably more work to build. In both cases the finished door should be several inches wider than and at least as long as the doorway it covers.

When the completed door has been taken inside the shelter and fitted over the doorway it should be thoroughly inspected and any gaps packed with wet leaves and mud. Remember, these same gaps that let in light now will also let in driving snow later. A stout branch cut to approximately two feet in length and having a Y-shaped crotch at one end can be used to hold the door in place from inside by wedging the Y under the top crosspiece and lightly kicking the bottom of the brace toward the door until it fits snugly against the front walls.

Unlike other shelters, which are heated by fires placed near their entrances, the dugout contains its own fireplace for heating and cooking in bad weather. The fireplace should be located against the back wall and situated so that sparks and hot coals that pop out of it during use won't damage the occupant's bed or equipment.

When a suitable location has been determined, begin by digging a squared hole into the wall approximately two feet in width by two feet long by two feet deep. The bottom of the fireplace should be at least six inches below the floor of the shelter to prevent hot coals from overflowing in the living space. Excess coals and ashes can be removed later using a flat slab of wood, and spread over the snow outside the shelter entrance to keep it from becoming slippery and dangerous to walk on.

The next step is to equip the fireplace with a chimney. This is best accomplished from the inside by using a knife to gouge a hole upward. Be sure to leave a minimum of one foot of insulating soil between the chimney hole and the inside wall of the shelter. Keep the inside diameter of the chimney as small as possible at first and widen it to a consistent six to eight inches afterward by ramming a log of the same size through it. Using a branch to widen the hole will ensure that the inside wall of the chimney is smooth and straight and will conduct smoke outside as efficiently as possible.

In use, the little fireplace will prove to be a very efficient heater, partly due to the well-insulated nature of the dugout shelter. Laying a small fire before turning in at night will heat the entire shelter until dawn on all but the coldest of nights. In fact, the occupant may find himself overheating and perspiring until he gets a feel for how much wood to use. Smoke should not be a problem except in high winds that produce a downdraft in the chimney. The amount of smoke produced can be kept to a minimum by using only dry wood from a small pile stored inside the shelter. Avoid using green wood altogether because burning it will coat the chimney wall with creosote, a flammable resin found in uncured wood. If the chimney does develop a downdraft, the problem can usually be remedied by cracking the door open a few inches.

The dugout is the most efficient and most comfortable of all shelters, but it's also the most difficult to build. Other extreme cold-weather shelters like the debris hut or the snow dugout are better choices for those who have a good chance of walking back to civilization. Spending a winter in snow country is hard on even the most skilled survivalist, because even if meat is abundant and he has a good supply of multivitamins, fat will be hard to come by. Fat may be the taboo of modern society, but it's a vitally important element of the woodsman's diet and without it he will be suffering from a form of malnutrition known as "rabbit starvation" before the spring thaw. But if conditions are such that they warrant toughing out the winter in one place, the dugout shelter is the most viable choice.

The Snow Dugout

The snow dugout is the best type of emergency shelter to build during a late winter blizzard when there's three to four feet of hardpack snow on the ground. A variation on the snow trench, it offers a bit more protection for a lot less work. I credit this shelter with saving my life when I was hit with a sudden blizzard during a photography excursion in February of 1984. The temperature dropped from a mild thirty degrees (Fahrenheit) to ten below in less than two hours, with wind chill factors that ranged between thirty below and forty below. I had to build a shelter quickly to escape that killing wind. Thanks to the snow dugout I was able to spend the next three days in relative comfort until the weather allowed me to leave.

The snow dugout will have particular appeal to snow-mobilers, cross-country skiers, and snowshoers, whose hobbies often take them into the deep woods in late winter. Even the fastest snowmobile can't make it to safety if it throws a track or blows the clutch, and slower-moving cross-country skiers are almost always poorly equipped and dressed to cope with a severe

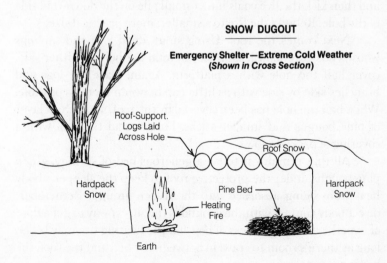

SNOW DUGOUT

Emergency Shelter—Extreme Cold Weather
(*Shown in Cross Section*)

Roof-Support.
Logs Laid
Across Hole

Roof Snow

Hardpack
Snow

Pine Bed

Heating
Fire

Hardpack
Snow

Earth

blizzard accompanied by high winds. Trappers and other snow-shoers are normally a bit better prepared to face cold weather, but even they recognize the danger of attempting to trek miles through a blizzard in high winds.

The beauty of the snow dugout lies not only in its effectiveness but in the speed with which it can be built. The first step is to lay a wood platform of heavy sticks side by side atop the snow. Then build a fire on top of this platform—a big fire. Like the Native Americans of old, I normally advocate small fires for cooking and heating, but in this case the survivalist should literally pour on the wood to create as large a blaze as he can manage without setting the forest afire.

As the fire gains strength it will begin to melt through the snow. Keep piling on the wood. Before long it will have melted through the hardpack and down to the ground. At this point the fire's heat will be focused directly against the snow walls surrounding it and the hole will rapidly increase in diameter, clearing a large patch of bare ground all around it.

When the hole in the hardpack has increased to approximately seven feet in diameter, allow the fire to die down to coals and then kick the live coals into a small pile on the downwind side of the hole. Rebuild the fire to a smaller, more practical size.

Next comes the roof. Using stout, dead logs and saplings whose ends extend at least a foot beyond the hole on either side, cover half the hole with a platform. Again, place the logs and branches side by side with as little gap between them as possible. When half the hole has been covered by the roof, add a thick layer of pine boughs and smaller sticks. Finally, seal the roof with a covering of packed snow.

All that remains is to lay a generous bed of springy, green pine boughs under the protective roof to keep the sleeper's body heat from being absorbed into the frozen ground. Remember, direct body contact with the ground is the surest way to get a dose of hypothermia, regardless of how hot the heating fire may be. So long as there's room to crawl in between the bed and the roof, the bed is not too thick.

As a late winter emergency shelter, the snow dugout has more going for it than the traditional snow trench or snow cave. The biggest advantage is the lack of work it takes to create it. The fire does most of the work and even keeps the victim warm while it's doing it. The roof keeps him dry and prevents him from being covered by falling snow, while being below the surface of the hardpack negates the wind chill factor. The icing on the cake is that the surrounding snow walls act as a very efficient omni-directional heat reflector, radiating the warmth of the campfire back toward the sleeping area from all directions. If you take refuge from a blizzard in the snow dugout, you can endure even the most vicious storm in relative comfort.

The stranded survivalist who has had the foresight to equip himself with a map and compass will in most cases decide to walk back to civilization rather than wait for someone to rescue him. In light of the fact that authorities are so quick to write off a missing woodsman as dead, I believe that taking charge of one's destiny by walking out is always the best choice if circumstances permit it.

A fast-moving, lightly-loaded woodsman who stops only to sleep will find it in his best interest to forego building any type of shelter at all if the weather will allow sleeping in the open with just a fire. In warm weather a thick bed of dried leaves, grass, ferns, or even pine needles will provide enough insulation and warmth to allow him a good night's sleep. If the weather is cold but clear he can lay his bed in a ravine or some other natural depression that offers good protection from the wind, using the sides as reflectors for his campfire.

But if the weather is foul, or if it suddenly turns foul, he will need to find shelter from the elements. Again, if he can avoid expending the energy necessary to build a conventional shelter he should do it. There are several types of emergency shelters that can be built quickly—usually in less than 30 minutes—that will provide adequate protection for the night.

The first of these is a very simple shelter that I've used several times in the past to escape cold, rainy weather for a night.

I call it the Emergency Dugout, a shelter that basically copies the dens used by foxes, badgers, and other animals who find conceal-ment and protection within the earth.

Emergency Shelters

The emergency dugout is a warm-weather shelter meant to be used in temperatures above freezing. Its construction is simple and quick; just find a hill with a steep slope on its leeward side and begin digging a low, horizontal slot wide enough and high enough to accommodate the sleeper's body. The excavated hole should be approximately two feet from bottom to top, seven feet in length, and should extend into the hillside about three feet. The floor of the shelter should be kept at least six inches above ground level to keep out running water. When the shelter is finished, with a thick bed of insulating material on the floor, there should be just enough room for the sleeper to crawl inside and have enough space to roll over. The back wall and ceiling will help to reflect the heat from a campfire placed at the entrance.

The emergency dugout is not an option for anyone who is even slightly claustrophobic. I've yet to have one of these shelters actually cave in, and if one of them did it would be little more than an irritation, but the confining nature of the emergency dugout will be more than enough to send anyone with a fear of small places into blind panic every time a bit of dirt falls from the ceiling. Remember skunks, opossums, marmots, and dozens of other creatures live in excavated burrows—when was the last time you heard about one of them suffocating in a cave-in?

Space Blanket and Polyurethane Shelters The space blanket also makes a handy emergency shelter. Being made of plastic, it will of course repel water, and the reflective foil coating will prevent most of a sleeper's body heat from being lost. There are a number of ways to rig the space blanket into a shelter, the simplest being just to cover up with it as one would with an ordinary blanket. Those who prefer to have a more roomy shelter can turn the space blanket into a tent by tying a length of cord between two trees at a height of three feet from the ground and draping the unfolded space blanket over it. Adjust the blanket so that the cord is in its center with an equal amount of material extending beyond it on either side. Spread one side of the blanket flat on the ground and weight it securely in place with logs, rocks or any other heavy objects. With one side firmly anchored, move to the other side and gently pull the blanket taut over the cord, anchoring it in place as you work along its length. The finished shelter will resemble a silvery pup tent and will provide a waterproof, reflective shelter for both the survivalist and his equipment. Bear in mind, however, that the space blanket isn't fire resistant and it will melt if placed too close to the campfire or struck by a hot coal. But it is as waterproof as any store-bought tent and will keep its occupant dry until morning.

Polyurethane plastic sheeting has been around for decades. This versatile material is waterproof, flexible in cold weather, available in heavy thicknesses, and downright cheap to buy. Like the space blanket, it can be used to make a variety of waterproof, windproof shelters, either by itself or anchored over a shelter frame. Polyurethane sheeting is available in a variety of widths and lengths (some quite large), but the colors are usually limited to black and clear. Of these, I recommend the clear because it's easier to spot from a passing plane and because it performs better than the black when used as a solar still (explained in detail in Chapter 4).

And the utility of polyurethane plastic isn't limited to just shelters. A piece of it set into a shallow hole and weighted all around on the ends can be filled with heated water and used as a washbasin for cleansing wounds or bathing. In a pinch polyurethane plastic can also be used to fashion a makeshift canteen, a campfire heat reflector, a poncho, a flotation device, an insect collector, or any number of other uses.

Natural Shelters The survivalist in need of shelter should never overlook those provided by nature. A skilled woodsman will expend as little energy as possible to get the job done, whatever it may be. Being lazy may be an unacceptable trait in civilization, but in civilization there's always a corner store, fast-food restaurant or stocked refrigerator available. In the wilderness one is always subject to the whims of nature, and it's not at all unusual for a woodsman who obtains his food from foraging or hunting to miss a few meals. Calories are precious, and need to be conserved whenever possible.

With this in mind, the energy-conscious survivalist should always be on the lookout for suitable natural shelters when stopping to rest for the night. Hibernation dens of wandering black bears are unoccupied from June through October, and these make excellent emergency shelters. Black bear dens are most often little more than an excavated hole under the roots of a large tree or in the side of a dirt bank. They won't be as large as some might think, because bruins know instinctively that a smaller den is easier to keep warm with body heat. Black bears will also hibernate inside large hollow logs—another possibility.

Caves are a form of natural shelter that at first glance might seem to be ideally suited to wilderness survival. In reality, however, caves are drafty, difficult to heat, and extremely smoky if the campfire is placed inside. A small, shallow cave will provide suitable shelter if a campfire is placed at the mouth with a reflector on its opposite side, but larger caves should be avoided in cold weather. Not only are larger caves drafty, but once the surrounding rock has cooled the inside will resemble a refrigerator.

Large fallen trees, especially pine trees, can often be used as emergency shelters. In most cases the branches will support the trunk and hold it off the ground. There may be enough room under the trunk for the survivalist to crawl in amongst the branches. If not, the branches can be trimmed from the trunk and used to fashion a roof, with the trunk providing the main roof support.

Remember, ingenuity and imagination are the foundation for all aspects of survival. The skilled outdoorsman can look at a tree and see shelter, tools, and weapons. Different types of terrain will have different features and anyone in need of shelter from a cold rain, blazing sun, or fierce winter storm will need to develop the ability to recognize these features for what they can be, not just what they are.

three

FIRE

The importance of fire to the woodsman in a survival situation cannot be exaggerated. Its most important function is as a source of heat to ward off debilitating hypothermia, but it also has tremendous value as a rescue signal, night light, cookstove, and even as a morale booster. The lost hunter or stranded canoeist who finds himself faced with the prospect of several cold nights in the wilderness will need all the cheer he can wring from his predicament, and a fireless camp is anything but cheerful. A bright, crackling blaze warms not only the body but the spirit as well.

Yet there are a surprising number of outdoorsmen who have little skill at getting a campfire started. I can recall sitting under a tree at a beachfront campground and watching in concealed amusement as two young men struggled mightily with their campfire for more than an hour without success. The two rummaged through their motor home and a nearby trash barrel to find bits of paper, cardboard and even styrofoam to use as tinder, but they just couldn't get the wood they'd stacked in the firepit to catch. I found it hard to supress a smile as I watched them rush to and fro atop the thick bed of dried pine needles that covered the campground. A handful of those pine needles would have started their fire with just the flick of a match.

There are many types of fire-starting tools and aids available to the woodsman, and anyone who plans to travel anywhere near a forest, particularly in cold weather, should be equipped to start a fire with at least one of them. For details on various fire-starting tools, see Chapter 1.

Tinder

The reason so many people have such a hard time lighting a campfire is impatience. In my experience, the most common mistake is trying to start the fire with sticks and branches that are too large to be ignited with the amount of heat one can produce with his fire-starting tools.

Seasoned woodsmen take a great amount of pride in their ability to start a campfire quickly in any weather. The trick is to be build the fire in stages, beginning with tinder and working to steadily larger pieces of wood as quickly as the fire and conditions will allow.

Tinder materials are readily available in nearly every type of environment. Probably the best of these is dry grass. Dry grass is extremely flammable and is the cause of the fast-moving wildfires that are the bane of folks living in the plains states. But to the woodsman, the volatility of dry grass is an advantage.

Under dry conditions a campfire or signal fire can be ignited very quickly by placing a couple of large handfuls of dry grass in a compact pile on the ground and laying several small, dry twigs on top in a circular, cone-shaped pattern. The touch of a lighted match will cause the grass to burst into flames, creating enough heat to ignite the twigs above it.

Under wet or rainy conditions dry grass is still one of the best tinder materials. But in this case the water must first be driven from the soaked fibers by evaporation. This will require fluffing the pile into a loose, airy mass that will allow the evaporating water vapor to escape. If the grass is very wet it will also help to use dry clothing or other pieces of woven fabric (like the dog rag mentioned in Chapter 1) to absorb as much water from the grass fibers as possible.

Dry grass can be used as tinder even in cold weather, with snow covering the ground. Remember, the things that were there before the first snowfall will still be there in the dead of winter, even though they may not be visible. Grass stems sticking up above the snow are like markers to the woodsman, telling him that there's tinder to be had beneath the surface of the snow. Grass dug from below the hardpack will be dry because snow and ice are not liquids, they're solids. Just be sure to shake off the ice crystals and snow before they have a chance to melt.

Dry pine needles also make an excellent tinder material and these are in abundance in most forested areas. They require a bit more heat to ignite than dry grass, but the pine resin contained in them burns with a hot, sputtering flame that lasts longer than that produced by burning grass.

Wet weather is less of a problem when using pine needles than it is with grass. Pine needles are more dense and less fibrous than grass, which makes them more resistant to moisture. But under wet conditions a tinder pile made from them should still be loose and airy to allow the individual needles to dry as they burn.

The fluff from dried cattail seedheads is a favorite tinder for many. These are abundant and highly visible year round in any place wet enough for cattails to grow. Even in mid winter, the hotdog-shaped brown seedheads can be spotted sticking up through the snow perched atop their slender stalks. Breaking up one or two of these seedheads will produce enough fluff to get a fire started, but in my experience cattail fluff has a tendency to smolder rather than flame, as does the very similar milkweed fluff. Both of these will work as tinder in a pinch, but if a hotter burning material is available, use it instead.

Dried moss, particularly the thick sphagnum moss found in swamps and bogs, is another favorite tinder material among experienced outdoorsmen. But again, I personally part company with them in this instance. Dried moss is hard to find in quantity because the places where it's most abundant are wet areas. And even though it will catch fire easily, it doesn't burn for very long or produce as much heat as other more readily available tinder.

Cotton balls like those sold in drug stores are excellent for use as tinder. These very fibrous, very flammable balls of fluff are inexpensive, light, and work well with matches, spark throwers, and the primitive but effective bow and drill. A cotton ball soaked with pine sap will work nearly as well as Trioxane for starting a fire, and if it's attached to the end of a branch it will also function very well as a torch.

Cloth fabric made from wool or cotton will work as tinder material in a pinch. In fact, the mountain men of old often carried pieces of rag for use as tinder with their steel and flint. Synthetic fabrics made from nylon or other petroleum-based materials are almost useles as tinder, but a piece of cotton flannel that has been well frayed will begin to smolder as soon as a spark hits it. I don't recommend sacrificing bits of clothing to start a campfire except in a dire emergency, but it wouldn't be a bad idea to include a bit of cotton cloth in one's survival kit in case suitable tinder isn't readily available.

Wood shavings are an excellent yet usually overlooked tinder material. Remember, the smaller the piece of wood, the easier it is to light. A pile of shavings whittled from a dry stick— preferably softwood—will ignite with just a match. A variation on this method is to split a few dozen toothpick-size splinters from the stick and lay them in a loose pile atop one another. Both of these techniques are equally effective, and either of them will light with a single match under dry conditions.

Birch bark is an old standby fire-making material recognized by most experienced outdoorsmen. Yellow, silver, and white "paper" birch trees are all easily identified by their curly, ragged-looking bark, which can often be peeled from the trunk in handfuls. All types of birch bark are suitable for starting a campfire, but the snow-white bark of the paper birch seems to work best. Birch bark is valuable because a match is all it takes to ignite it into a hot, sputtering flame that will burn for up to several minutes.

Over the years it's become a habit with me to stop at birch trees I pass and fill a spare pocket with the flammable bark. It's a good habit and one that I very much recommend to the outdoor traveler. Few of nature's fire-starting materials are as effective or as available as birch bark, and having a pocketful of the stuff assures that he will be equipped to start a fire any time without having to go look for tinder.

Many woodsmen believe that birch bark is valuable as an emergency fire-starting material because it will burn even when it's wet. That is absolutely not true, and those who claim it is have obviously never tested the veracity of their belief. Birch bark does repel water to a degree—which is one of the reasons it was so widely used by Native Americans in the construction of canoes and wanigans—but it will absorb significant amounts of water after prolonged exposure. The survivalist who needs to start a fire in a steady rain is best advised not to waste his time with soggy birch bark.

Dried bracken ferns and leaves are abundant in forested areas from spring until the snow covers them in winter. Neither of these are very good for starting fires, because bracken ferns tend to blaze and then go out very quickly, and leaves will usually just smolder, making it necessary to find a more steady-burning tinder material. A handful of dried bracken ferns tossed into an already burning fire will cause it to flare brightly for a few seconds, and can be handy for chasing off nosy animals, but neither leaves nor ferns make very good tinder material.

Fire-Starting Basics

The first step in starting a campfire is to find a suitable location. When using a shelter, the fire should always be located directly in front of the entrance, but at a distance that will keep flames or sparks from setting the shelter afire. In windy weather both the fire and shelter should be located on the lee side of a hill or in thickly wooded terrain to help block air currents that can blow hot sparks into the woods and create a wind chill factor in cold weather. As an added precaution, all combustible debris should be scraped or kicked away from the campfire for at least three feet in all directions.

The next step is to create a firepit. Popping coals are a fact of life when one is burning any dry softwood, especially pine, and a firepit is necessary to contain as many of them as possible without blocking the heat from the fire. For this same reason any campfire should be kept as small as possible. An old Indian saying states that a white man's camp can be identified by the size of its fire, which is always too big. From what I've seen that adage still holds true today. Signal fires are naturally quite large and bright, but campfires should be kept small and manageable.

The traditional method of creating a firepit is to place large stones around its circumference. Stones tend to absorb and radiate heat from the fire long after it has burned down to coals. The survivalist can use these heated stones to keep warm through the night by wrapping one or two of them in a dog rag or a piece of clothing and placing the bundle at the foot of his bed as a toe-warmer. Typically, if a person's feet get cold, his whole body will feel chilled.

Stones are often hard to come by in the thick humus of a forest or swamp, but large stones can often be found in the beds of fast-moving streams. *Never* subject stones taken from any stream or other body of water to the heat of a campfire. As hard as stone is, it's still a porous material, and will absorb water after a period of time. A campfire burns with far more heat than most folks realize, and within just a few minutes it can heat a waterlogged stone to the point where the moisture trapped inside it becomes rapidly expanding steam vapor. In some cases the steam will be created faster than it can escape and internal pressures will mount until the stone explodes. Rain-wet stones are safe to use, as are any other stones found on what is normally dry land, but using waterlogged stones to surround a campfire is asking for trouble.

When stones are hard to come by, as they will be in most forested areas, the woodsman can contain his fire with an excavated firepit. The excavated firepit is even better than the stone fire-pit for containing hot sparks because there are no gaps in the wall surrounding the coal bed. This firepit is constructed by excavating a shallow hole in the earth about eighteen inches in diameter and four inches deep. The soil taken from the hole is used to form a low wall around the outside. The fire is then set in the center of the firepit hole. If one or two large stones are available, they can be fitted into the earthen wall for later use as toe-warmers.

The next step is to lay the fire itself, and this is where the inexperienced woodsman most often has difficulty. Begin by placing the tinder material, which can be dried grass, birch bark, Trioxane, or any other actively combustible material, in the center of the firepit. If the fire is to be built atop snow, place a platform of dry sticks beneath the tinder to keep it from melting into the snow and extinguishing itself. But don't light the tinder just yet.

Next, lay a cone-shaped teepee of small, dry sticks all around the circumference of the tinder pile so that they come together and support one another about eight inches above the floor of the firepit. The teepee method of arranging kindling will ensure that a sizeable air gap exists between the tinder pile

STARTING A FIRE WITH WET WOOD—*TEEPEE METHOD*

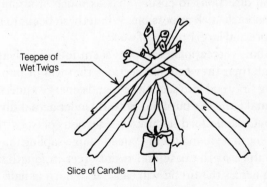

Teepee of Wet Twigs

Slice of Candle

and the sticks above it, as well as between the kindling sticks themselves.

When starting a fire using wet wood, or in the rain, the teepee method of arranging the kindling is the only real choice. When the woods are wet one should use sticks for the teepee that are as small in diameter as possible. The burning tinder, Trioxane bar or section of candle will provide enough heat to dry and ignite the lower layer of sticks, which in turn will dry and ignite the upper layers of sticks that serve as a roof to protect the lower pieces of kindling from rain.

When the woods are wet, avoid using small branches found lying on the ground to start a fire. These will be the wettest pieces of wood in the forest, and may even be waterlogged. They can be used after the fire is coaxed to a blaze, but starting the fire should be done using dry, dead twigs that are still attached to their trees. Since these branches are suspended, rain will tend to run off of them and they will begin to dry in the open air immediately after the rain stops. Branches and twigs found lying on the ground will absorb and trap water beneath them, sometimes for days.

Refrain from adding more wood as soon as the teepee begins to blaze. The fire is still at a delicate stage and adding too much wood too soon can extinguish it. Wait until the teepee begins to cave in on itself and hot coals fall off the burning twigs. At this point the fire builder can add longer sticks of a slightly larger diameter, laying them across the disintegrating teepee from all directions to ensure that as much of an air gap exists between each stick as possible. When these begin to burn freely, add more and larger pieces of wood.

Many recreational campers seem to feel obligated to chop or break their firewood into sections that will fit into the firepit. Cutting firewood into sections expends energy unnecessarily and won't make the fire burn any better. Under actual survival conditions one should feed his fire with sections of wood that are the same length he found them. A dead maple sapling may be several inches thick at the base and twenty feet in length. Laying the sapling across the firepit will cause it to burn in half. The halves can in turn be laid across the firepit where they too will be burned in half, or they can be fed into the fire as the ends burn off. Before long the entire sapling will have been consumed. Surviving in the wilderness is rough under the best conditions, so never waste energy performing a task that can be avoided or accomplished with less work.

Matches and other fire-starting aids are precious, and must be conserved to make them last as long as possible, particularly if circumstances dictate that one remain in one location for an indefinite period of time. Since it wouldn't be economical or wise to build a new fire each day, bank the fire at night or whenever leaving the campsite for any length of time.

Banking a fire essentially means reducing it to a slow-burning, relatively cool bed of smoldering coals. The fire stays alive but doesn't flame. A properly banked fire will remain viable for up to twenty-four hours, and can even resist a mild rain or light dusting of snow.

Bank a campfire by first letting it burn down to a bed of glowing coals. Then scrape the coals into a compact pile in the center of the firepit. The last step is to lay two large-diameter logs side by side and directly on top of the coals. The logs will be too large and too thick to burst into flame, but the coals will cause them to smolder from the underside where they'll have a degree of protection from the elements. Eventually the coals will eat into the underside of the logs until a wide gap exists between them, and the coals will die from lack of fuel. But if the logs are thick and the coals are hot to begin with, the fire will remain at a slow idle throughout the day, while the survivalist tends to other important chores.

Types of Fire

So far we've covered fire in general, but there are several different types of fire the survivalist can use for a variety of purposes. The more multi-functional any tool of survival is—or can be made—the more valuable it becomes, and fire is no exception.

The Heating Fire The heating fire is probably the one of most immediate importance in cold or wet weather. Fires used for heating don't really have to be large, but they do have tall flames. These high flames not only provide a maximum of warmth, but throw a significant amount of light as well. The pieces of wood used to fuel a heating fire are necessarily of a large diameter to prevent the fire from burning down too quickly, and that also means a hot bed of coals.

A fire used for warmth or light is created using the same basic teepee method employed for starting the fire, except in this case a good bed of coals already exists and the wood used to form the teepee is thicker. The heating fire is omnidirectional, throwing both warmth and light in all directions, so its energy should always be channeled through the use of at least one reflector, and preferably three.

The Hot Bed The hot bed is an old mountain man's invention that was once used quite extensively by them to help keep warm during cold winter nights in the open, when a five-point wool horse blanket was the standard bedroll. Anyone who has ever slept in the open air on even a warm summer night can attest to the amount of body heat lost. The hot bed helped to counteract this by providing a constant, if steadily diminishing, source of heat from below. Properly constructed, it will keep a person warm throughout the night in very cold weather (so long as the air is still).

Preparation of the hot bed is simple but can best be accomplished with the help of a small shovel or entrenching tool. The first step is to build a long, hot fire that measures approximately four feet wide by seven feet in length. The fire should be fueled until a solid bed of red coals is formed and allowed to burn down. The glowing bed of coals is then covered with a layer of loose dirt or sand at least four inches thick and tamped down as much as possible. An alternate method is to excavate a shallow, body-length depression and then shovel the hot coals into it, covering them with the dirt taken from the excavation. Both methods are equally effective, but the former requires a bit less effort.

The dirt-covered hot bed is well insulated and can be used without further work, but my own experience has been that the normal rolling and shifting of position that occurs during sleep is apt to scrape away the protective earth and expose the sleeper to a rude, painful awakening. As protection against this I recommend laying a thin layer of pine boughs or leafy branches over the dirt. A poncho thrown over the dirt will also work to keep the dirt in place, but keep in mind that doing so also exposes the poncho to the possibility of being burned.

The Cooking Fire Cooking over an open fire requires a bit more skill than one might think. The most common error made by campers is in trying to cook over a flaming campfire. This is dangerous to both the person cooking the food and to the food itself. A campfire produces far more heat than an electric or gas range, and food cooked over its flames will char on the outside before it can be cooked on the inside.

The easiest way to convert a campfire to a cooking fire is to simply push the burning wood to one side of the firepit and scrape together a good hot bed of coals. A bed of live, red-hot coals will provide a flat and stable surface to set a canteen cup or mess tin without exposing the cook to dangerous open flames. The coals will eventually cool as their heat is transfered to the metal container, but they will usually be sufficient to boil water or cook food. The life of coals can also be prolonged by setting the cooking container on a platform of two or three short, thick sticks laid on top of the coals about an inch apart.

The spit is a traditional way of cooking birds and small animals over a fire. This method doesn't require the use of any cooking utensils, and is the easiest method of preparing wild game in a survival situation. The spit begins with two forked sticks set vertically into the ground on either side of the firepit. The straight, bottom end of each stick should be pushed at least six inches into the soil, and both should be stable enough not to fall over under the weight of the loaded spit. The crotch of these support sticks should be approximately two feet above the floor of the firepit. The sticks should be made from green wood, although dry wood can be used as long as the sticks are placed far enough from the fire to keep them from burning.

The spit itself should always be constructed of green wood at least an inch in diameter and long enough to extend beyond the crotch of either support stick a minimum of four inches on either side. The spit is sharpened on one end and threaded through the rib cage, and through the pelvis, for small mammals. Small birds or fish are simply speared through the ribs and slid over the spit. Larger fish are spitted by piercing them at an angle near the tail, bending the body into a U and piercing again near the head.

When selecting a length of wood for use as a spit, be sure to avoid all species of pine or cedar. These resinous softwoods may have a pleasant smell, but the taste they impart to cooked foods is distinctly unpleasant. Pine burns hot and fast, which is fine for starting a fire or even heating water in a container, but it should never be used for cooking or smoking meat.

In practice, a spitted animal or fish is suspended over a low fire or hot bed of coals by setting the end of the spit into the crotch of the support stick at either end and sliding the meat to the center of the spit. The fire beneath it should always be kept as low as possible and the meat turned frequently. Cook all wild meat or fish thoroughly. The addition of green birch, aspen, or maple will cause the fire to smoke and help to sweeten the meat as it cooks.

Wilderness cooking is one of the activities in which the leather work gloves mentioned in Chapter 1 will prove very useful. Cloth gloves, especially ski gloves, should never be used as protection from the heat of a cooking fire or for handling hot utensils, but leather gloves offer very good shielding when working around the fire. They aren't impervious to fire and common sense should be exercised to prevent burns, yet they will allow the campfire cook to reach into the firepit and quickly remove a canteen cup filled with boiling water without injury.

The Signal Fire The signal fire is unique among the types of fire used by the woodsman because of its large size and high visibility. It has to be large and bright to attract as much attention as possible from as many miles away as is needed. Unfortunately, the amount of heat and sparks generated by the signal fire pretty much precludes it from being located anywhere near a shelter. In fact, the open ridges and bluffs that are so ideal for setting a signal fire are probably the worst places to set up camp.

To be as effective as possible, the signal fire must also be as large as it can safely be, and will thus require a great deal of wood. It behooves those in need of rescue to use a signal fire sparingly and only when there exists a good chance that it will be spotted by a passing plane, boat, or hunting party. With this in mind, the signal fire should be pre-assembled in a way that will cause it to flame quickly with the touch of a match.

Construction of the ready-made signal fire begins with a hot-burning tinder, such as dried grass, topped by a large teepee of dried twigs and sticks—preferably of a softwood. Next comes a larger teepee of heavier branches about six feet in length. The two teepees will help keep the tinder dry by forming a roof over it. When the survivalist spots a plane or some other potential rescuer, he lights the tinder, which lights the smaller teepee of sticks. The flames from the smaller teepee will in turn ignite the larger teepee, sending a brilliant pyre of flame into the night to a height of ten feet or more.

Assuming that both tinder and wood are dry, the signal fire will flame up very quickly, usually within minutes. But be warned: the larger teepee will consume itself from the bottom up and can be expected to burn for no more than fifteen minutes before collapsing to one side. For this reason the signal fire must be located in a place where there's no danger of causing a forest fire when it falls over.

During the hours of darkness a signal fire can be seen for miles, but in daylight the flames fade to near obscurity. Watchers who man firetowers know that flames from even the hottest forest fire are difficult to see in full daylight, but a plume of smoke against the sky is highly visible. Armed with this knowledge, one can continue to signal during the day by building a large, hot fire and then partially smothering it with a layer of damp, rotting wood or wet leaves. The coals will have enough heat to burn the damp material but not enough to ignite it, and the fire will smoke heavily.

WATER

An average human can function well for long periods of time without eating, but none of us can survive more than four or five days without water, and even less if the weather is hot. The combined effects of too much sun and too little water can be especially devastating to the individual who must travel.

Waterborne Diseases

Fortunately, most areas of North America have an abundance of water. But unfortunately, many water sources have become polluted, or contain parasites that can put the strongest of us out of commission, sometimes in just a few hours. In most cases these diseases are the result of parasitic infestation by nematodes and trematodes, two families whose members include such unsavory creatures as hookworms, pinworms, tapeworms, and other organisms that live in the host's internal organs. There are literally hundreds of thousands of species of these tiny animals living in the soil and water worldwide. Eighty thousand of them are known to parasitize vertebrate animals and more than fifty species are dangerous to man.

The past decade has seen an increase in the numbers of hikers and campers who have fallen victim to parasitic infestation. Ironically, many of those cases have been created by the ignorance of the victims. It seems that many of them have a tendency to defecate in water, a trait that probably developed as the result of too many years using modern plumbing. Human fecal matter is perhaps the most likely to carry infectious organisms, and the growing number of people who frequent the wilderness has made even the once pristine waters of the Rocky Mountains a source of disease.

Parasitic nematodes and trematodes are a danger for which every woodsman should prepare. The immature organisms are often carried inside the bodies of freshwater snails, whose browsing habits cause them to become attached to water plants. Still others are free-living in water. When they are ingested by a suitable host, they attach to an internal organ and begin to mature. Depending on the type of parasite, they may attach to the stomach, intestines, liver, lungs, or even the heart, where they will feed until maturity, sometimes killing the host.

Giardia, a parasitic infection that has gained considerable attention over the past few years in North America, is one of the most dangerous because its symptoms mimic those of intestinal influenza. Fever and cramps are accompanied by a chronic and persistent diarrhea that can and in many cases has weakened and dehydrated its victims to the point of death.

Beaver fever is a disease that was well known among trappers in the 1800s. They may not have known what caused it, but those old-timers knew that drinking untreated water from the downstream side of a beaver dam, or from the beaver pond itself, would frequently cause the drinker to become seriously ill for several days.

Beaver fever is caused by the beavers' habit of defecating almost exclusively in the water around their home. Beaver ponds are favored drinking spots for most animals, and man appears to be the only animal susceptible to this disease. Beaver fever is almost never fatal, but the chills and fever associated with it can be indirectly dangerous to someone stranded in the woods, especially in cold weather.

Typhoid (*Salmonella typhosa*) is another bacterial infection that one should guard against. Dangerous only to man, it is just one of several harmful salmonella bacteria that might be found in the stagnant water of swamps or ponds. Typhoid itself is usually transmitted by contact with the feces or urine of infected individuals, but it might also be carried by animals who are themselves immune.

The incubation period for the typhoid bacteria is usually ten to twelve days, and symptoms may vary from no reaction at all to flu-like fever, constipation, and nosebleeds, and may cause death. Military personnel are routinely vaccinated against typhoid during basic training, so those who served in any branch of the armed forces will likely be immune. But there are other related bacteria like those that cause septicemia and gastroenteritis that may exist in stagnant waters. These are not as directly life-threatening as typhoid, but can be equally dangerous because they will make it impossible to perform the tasks necessary to stay alive.

Chemical pollutants have found their way into nearly every body of water on Earth. It's a fact of life that fish now contain high levels of mercury in their tissues and many states now recommend against eating them. Recreational boaters have dumped tons of lead into our lakes over the years, and the sulfuric acid from millions of unleaded automobile exhausts has created the insidious acid rain problem with which we're all familiar.

Most of these pollutants are not immediately dangerous, and short of distilling all drinking water, all of them are unavoidable. But in most cases exposure can be kept to a minimum. Utility companies, for example, are noted for their use of herbicides to keep power lines free of undergrowth. Farmers use both herbicides and insecticides, and the once common practice of oiling dirt roads to keep the dust down is still haunting us. Snow and rain runoff from all of these and more washes chemical contaminants into streams and lakes that may be dozens of miles from the source. It pays to become familiar with the area you'll be in to avoid ingesting high concentrations of these chemicals.

Some diseases aren't directly contracted from drinking water but rather from insects that breed in the water, namely the more than sixteen hundred recognized species of mosquito that exist throughout the world. During warm weather mosquitoes can be found in heavy concentrations near water throughout North America. Considering their numbers (a single inland lake may be home to millions), mosquito-borne diseases are quite rare in the northern regions. Nonetheless, it pays to be aware of the insects' potential for transmitting disease.

Malaria is a disease most often associated with subtropical and tropical regions of the world, but it also occurs with surprising frequency in the north. In Michigan alone there are approximately fifty new cases reported each summer. Malaria is caused by a single-celled organism of the genus *Plasmodium*, which attacks the liver and red blood cells of its host. Malaria is transmitted by members of the Anopheles family of mosquitoes, and there is no cure, although the victim will eventually develop a resistance to the chills and fever that are the trademark of malarial attacks.

Encephalitis is an inflammation of the brain that can cause dizziness, sleepiness, double vision, gastrointestinal problems, or even a coma, depending on the type of virus that infects the host. An outbreak of highly contagious and often fatal equine encephalitis in the early 1980s panicked several northeastern states. This and several other types of encephalitis are transmitted by mosquitoes belonging to the Aedes and Culex families, as well as certain ticks.

Dengue, or breakbone fever, is a viral infection caused by the Aedes mosquito. The disease is marked by muscle soreness, fever, weakness, and severe pain behind the eyes. It's almost never fatal and will usually pass within a week.

Yellow fever is another disease usually associated with tropical climates, but in the nineteenth century more than half a million cases were reported in the continental United States, most of them in Maryland and New York. This disease is often fatal, and though it has been pretty much eradicated in the northern states, the potential for an outbreak still exists.

Water Purification

The easiest method of killing infectious organisms in water is by heating it to the boiling point (212 degrees Fahrenheit). Boiling will kill any harmful organisms that might be living in the water, making it safe for cooking, drinking, or bathing wounds.

Authorities sometimes disagree about how long water should be boiled before it becomes absolutely safe for human consumption. Some say that it's safe to drink as soon as it reaches the boiling point; others recommend that it be boiled for several minutes; and one magazine writer even went as far as saying that water was safe to drink only if it had been boiled for twenty minutes. I suspect this last individual was a bit phobic about germs, because twenty minutes of boiling will not only kill any living creature in existence, but will evaporate most of the water as well. In real life, four or five minutes is sufficient to remove any danger.

But keep in mind that the amount of heat required to bring water to boiling will decrease as the elevation increases. Water heated at or below sea level will feel extremely hot before it reaches the boiling point, but water heated on a high mountainside may boil furiously and still not be too hot to touch. At high elevations—and thus decreased atmospheric pressure—it may be necessary to cover the container with a loose-fitting lid to artificially increase the pressure against the water.

A common complaint from those who drink boiled water is that it tastes flat and somewhat metallic. The reason for this phenomenon is that boiling removes most of the oxygen from water. There are two ways to at least partially alleviate this problem. One is to boil the water with a large piece of charcoal (taken from the campfire bed) in the bottom of a metal container, and the other is to shake the cooled water vigorously in a half-filled, closed canteen to re-aerate it. The water will still taste boiled, but much of the flatness will be gone.

In times past it was common practice to add liquor to water in an attempt to purify it. The logic was that if alcohol could be used to sterilize wounds and surgical instruments, wouldn't it work just as well to sterilize water? The truth is that alcohol doesn't purifty water, because the concentration required to kill all the harmful organisms that might be living in it would also poison the person who drank the water. Alcohol, especially in the form of individually packaged prep pads, is a handy item to have in the first-aid kit, but it should never be relied upon as a water purifier.

Chlorine is another water purification chemical that has only limited value in the woods. In urban areas chlorine is routinely added to water to dispatch any cholera or typhoid bacteria that might be living in it. Chlorine is an effective germ-killer, but the woodsman will be confronted with organisms not found in any city's water supply. Chlorine-releasing Halazone tablets were tested by the military more than a decade ago, but were rejected because chlorine in a concentration that's safe for human consumption simply won't kill all the infectious or parasitic organisms found in the wilderness.

Iodine, best known as a local antiseptic for cuts and abrasions, is the water purifier of choice for both military personnel and civilian woodsmen the world over. It is highly toxic to every living thing, but the difference between medicine and poison often lies in the dosage. A human being can safely consume water that has enough of the antiseptic in it to destroy any form of life it might carry. The one drawback is that water treated with iodine will have a metallic, slightly astringent taste some folks find objectionable, but there's no avoiding that as yet.

Iodine tablets are available commercially at most outfitters and camping supply stores, at an average retail price of around two dollars for 100 tablets. Each of these small red tablets is meant to disinfect a one-quart canteen of water, which translates into twenty-five gallons of purified water per bottle of tablets, enough to keep an individual supplied with potable water for more than three months.

The one problem with iodine tablets is their shelf (or kit) life—in most cases they'll need to be replaced long before the tablets have been used up. The normal bumps, jars, and vibrations that any survival kit is likely to experience will cause the tablets to disintegrate into powder over a period of several months, especially if the kit is carried in an off-road vehicle. The screw-top bottles that the tablets are usually packaged in are also notorious for admitting just enough moisture to cause the tablets inside to crumble, reducing them to powder.

A simple solution to this problem can be found in ordinary liquid iodine, available for less than a dollar at most drug stores. Many doctors now recommend against using iodine to disinfect wounds because it also destroys skin cells, but it's still the best water purification method available, short of boiling. Two to three drops from the dropper attached to the bottle cap will be sufficient to kill any infectious organisms that might be living in the water without exposing the survivalist to any toxic side effects.

Whether using liquid iodine or iodine tablets, the first step is to fill the canteen. If the water source is a stream, point the open mouth of the canteen downstream at a slight angle, and hold it at least three inches below the surface of the water. This will prevent an excess of floating debris from being sucked into the canteen. If the source is a lake or pond, simply hold the canteen in a vertical position with the mouth three inches below the surface of the water but far enough off the bottom to avoid stirring up silt. In both cases, when the canteen stops bubbling it will be full.

Next, dump out just enough water to empty the neck of the canteen and add one iodine tablet or two drops of iodine—three drops if the water was taken from a very stagnant pool or lake. Never exceed three drops, regardless of how dirty or smelly the water may be. Screw the cap on tightly and shake the filled canteen vigorously to circulate the iodine. Wait at least fifteen minutes to be certain that all organisms are dead. Uncap the canteen and slosh the purified water over the mouth and outer threads of the canteen neck. Use a little more of the same water to wash out the canteen cap and any other surfaces that might come in contact with the lips.

Many people associate silt and floating debris with "dirty" water, but the amount of mud, silt or wood particles in a body of water has no bearing on how safe it is for human consumption. Nor does its smell, even though it's always advisable to avoid drinking fetid water.

But whether it contains harmful organisms or not, murky water should not be drunk because the human body's natural reaction to it will be to choke or even vomit, neither of which will do the survivalist any good. When circumstances dictate that silt-filled water must be used for drinking or cooking, always strain it prior to purification to remove sediment and suspended particles that may make you ill.

This is where the "dog rag" mentioned in Chapter 1 comes into play. Dogs rags were carried by Special Forces personnel in Vietnam, where they were employed as wash cloths, tourniquets, arm slings, emergency bandages, sweat bands, and water strainers. Like many valuable tools of survival, the dog rag is simple and straightforward. It consists of nothing more than a large square of cloth, preferably flannel or jersey, measuring three to four feet across.

To use the dog rag as a water strainer, first stretch a corner of it across the open canteen mouth and hold it snugly in place while filling the canteen. This will filter out most of the sediment that might otherwise get into the canteen. Next, stretch a clean portion of the dog rag across the open top of the canteen cup and pour the once-strained contents back through it and into the cup. The water in the canteen cup will now be free of all but the most microscopic particles and organisms. Pour some of the twice-strained water back into the canteen to rinse out any large particles that might have gotten through when it was filled, empty the canteen on the ground and refill it with the remainder of the water from the canteen cup. The strained water can now be purified by boiling or with iodine.

Portable water filters made their way into the outdoor market in the early 1980s and they appear to have had a good reception from recreational backpackers and hikers. These filters generally use a strong hydraulic sucking action to draw water through a ceramic or charcoal filter and into a reservoir, although a few are gravity-operated. According to company claims, some of these filters are capable of filtering out organisms and sediment down to 0.2 microns, and will even remove chemicals, leaving the user with clean, drinkable water.

There are several types and makes of water filter on the market, including a tube that reportedly can purify water just by sucking contaminated water through it the way one would an ordinary drinking straw. Prices vary with the type and size of filter, but the Swiss-made Katadyn Filter is probably the best of these and retails for around $240. Some are less expensive, ranging from twenty dollars to $150, so the survivalist should shop around to find the model that best fits his needs and budget.

The Solar Still "Water, water everywhere, and not a drop to drink." No doubt this bit of poetry, which has had so much meaning to so many shipwrecked sailors, was at least part of the inspiration behind the solar still. No one seems to know exactly who invented this wonderfully simple and efficient water distillation device, but its utility can be seen in the fact that every lifeboat and liferaft in the US Navy is equipped with several self-contained units. Not only will the solar still distill and purify tainted water, it will also gather as much as a quart of the valuable liquid per day, even in the most arid desert.

Like all the best survival tools, the solar still is simple both in principle and in fact. Anyone who's ever noticed the condensation inside a plastic-draped pile of lumber or inside their tent on a sunny morning has seen the theory behind the solar still in action.

THE SOLAR STILL
(Shown in Cross Section)

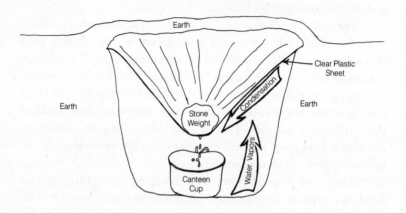

All that's needed to construct one in the wild is a sheet of clear poluyurethane plastic about four feet square, a rock, a shallow hole, a canteen cup and about twelve hours.

Here's how it works: first find or create a shallow depression in the ground. The diameter of the hole should be as large as possible but still small enough for the plastic sheet to cover it with about ten inches to spare on all sides. It's important that the plastic be able to cover the depression entirely without being stretched tight. The depth of the depression should be about one foot in the center and may be tapered downward slightly on the sides.

But don't cover the hole with the plastic just yet. The next step is to set the canteen cup—or tin can or any other watertight container—upright in the center of the depression. This container will act as the collection reservoir.

With the container in place at the bottom of the depression, cover the top of the hole with the plastic sheet. Weight all four corners of the plastic sheet with large stones, logs, or other weights to keep it from slipping and if necessary, fold the corners double and drive a small wooden stake through each one and into the ground. When the corners are secured, add more weights around the perimeter and seal the edges with a layer of loose dirt. With everything in place, the plastic sheet should sag slightly, but not more than six inches.

The final step is to place a fist-size stone in the center of the plastic sheet and directly over the opening of the container at the bottom of the depression.

As the name implies, the solar still uses the energy of the sun to condense and distill water, although it will operate with decreased efficiency under overcast skies so long as the weather remains warm. The rays of the sun will pass through the clear plastic sheet to heat the ground beneath it. As the ground heats, the moisture contained in it will evaporate and the vapors will begin to rise upward until they're stopped by the airtight plastic sheet. Trapped thus, the water vapors will saturate the confined air inside the hole and condense into droplets against the underside of the plastic sheet. When the vapors change from a gas to a liquid they become subject to the force of gravity. But there's also a strong molecular bond between the water droplets and the plastic which makes them tend to stick to the plastic. As these two forces strive to overcome one another the droplets will follow the path of least resistance, sliding downhill along the surface of the plastic until they reach the apex of the cone you've created, directly beneath the weight in the center of the plastic sheet. Here they will merge into the large drops that finally must obey the force of gravity and fall into the container below.

A major advantage of the solar still is that it operates at peak efficiency during the heat of the day, a time when the desert-traveling survivalist should be resting. But bear in mind that when the sun rises in the desert it gets very hot very quickly and any moisture near the surface will be vaporized within the first two hours. Since the desert survivalist will be walking during the cold night hours and holed up under any available shade to sleep away the heat of the day, his first act before dawn should be to construct at least one, and preferably two solar stills. Also remember that the solar still not only collects water but distills it as well, so the survivalist can use it to recycle his own urine into drinking water. Just be sure to urinate in the hole *before* placing the canteen cup at the bottom of it.

Water Sources

Few places in North America are completely devoid of water, and none are without moisture in some form—the ability of the solar still to collect water from the air and ground is proof of that. But some water sources aren't obvious, while others may not be wise to use. The following information will help you remain well hydrated and healthy during a stay in the wilderness.

Freshwater springs are always a good bet when one needs clean drinking water. Springs are often quite plentiful in wooded lowlands, and especially near rivers or larger streams. They can normally be found on ground several feet higher than the streams they feed into, and in many cases the source will be right in the side of a seemingly dry hill. Springs are always small and fast-flowing, which precludes infestation by snails or other parasite carriers, and because the water is filtered through millions of tons of earth, rock and gravel, the only impurities left in it are natural minerals.

When taking water from a freshwater spring, always go to its point of origin, the place where it comes out of the ground. This water will be cold and clean enough to drink or cook with just as it is. The same may not hold true farther downstream.

Rain has always been a good water source, and it still is, even though pollution and toxic emissions have added chemicals to it that it never contained before. Rainwater is at least as clean as urban tapwater, and is definitely a safer bet than swamp water, so the survivalist should be prepared to take advantage of this boon from above.

The easiest method of collecting rainwater is to use a rubberized poncho or plastic sheet set into a shallow depression in the ground. This will form a small watertight basin that can hold more than three gallons of water.

Snow is safe for use as drinking water, even though it contains the same chemical pollutants as modern rain. The biggest drawback to using melted snow as a source of water is that its volume is about three times as great as water; a gallon bucket filled with snow will yield just over a quart of water.

When facing a survival situation in cold weather, never eat snow. The survivalist who has spent three or four days in frozen, snow covered terrain will find his body adapting quickly, acclimating itself to the cold. But this change isn't without cost. As his body adapts it will burn more energy and require more calories to sustain a normal temperature. Calories and fat are vitally important to someone stranded in cold weather, and eating snow will only make his body work even harder. Always melt snow or ice with the campfire, and always try to drink warmed or hot water in sub-freezing temperatures.

Dew is an often overlooked source of water in arid areas. Even the most sun-scorched desert has some degree of humidity, but during the heat of the day that moisture will be in the form of vapor, which is useless to a thirsty traveler. At night the cloudless skies that are the trademark of desert areas will do nothing to prevent the day's heat from escaping into the atmosphere, and temperatures will drop precipitously. The sudden drop in temperature will cause the water vapors to condense and gather on the surface of rocks where they can be collected with a dog rag. When the dog rag becomes saturated with dew, simply wring it out into the canteen cup and gather more. A full day's supply of water can be gathered in this way. The dewfall will be at its maximum during the early morning hours—from 3:00 AM to sunrise—and this is the best time to gather dew.

Like people, plants need water to live, and like people, their tissues contain a large percentage of water. All of us have heard about how aboriginal peoples obtain liquid from jungle lianas, desert cacti, or underground tubers, but the truth is that all non-toxic soft-bodied plants and their roots can be used to provide a thirst-quenching juice.

To obtain liquid from a plant, first crush it between the palms with a rolling action, as if rolling clay into a ball. When the plant takes on a wet, fibrous consistency raise the hand slightly overhead, tip your head back, point your extended thumb at your open mouth and squeeze hard. The juices forced from the crushed plant will flow downward to drip off the end of your thumb and into your mouth.

The same can be done with roots, but as they're harder they will usually need to be reduced to a pile of shavings before any liquid can be squeezed from them using hand pressure. When traveling through an arid environment, bear in mind that some species of plants die back after the rainy season, but the roots will remain viable and are often a good source of water. A withered plant lying on the surface of the ground or an apparently dead twig sticking up may indicate a live, dormant root beneath the surface. But always use caution and never drink liquid from any plant that you can't positively identify as non-toxic.

Knowing the location of active water holes is absolutely vital to anyone traveling through desert country. As a service to travelers, desert states maintain a number of water tanks and wind-powered well pumps in the back country. Maps giving the location of each of these are available from state fish and game agencies and anyone driving, hiking, or riding through the desert should have one for their area. It's also a good idea to begin the journey with as much water as you can carry, just in case.

The water from a stranded vehicle's radiator can also be used as a source of drinking water, but only after distillation. Never, ever attempt to drink the water from the cooling system of any vehicle as it comes out of the radiator. Triethylene glycol, the active ingredient in modern antifreeze/coolant is extremely toxic, and ingesting even small amounts of it can cause immediate kidney failure, convulsions, and death. But again, the solar still is capable of purifying the coolant into drinking water by separating water vapors from the heavier glycol. As an added precaution, I recommend distilling vehicle coolant twice, using two separate solar stills. When the container at the bottom of the first solar still becomes full, dump the once-purified water into the soil at the bottom of the second solar still for a final distillation. Thoroughly wipe the inside of the collection container used in the first solar still clean with a dry cloth or sand to remove any traces of coolant. Double-distillation may not be necessary to purify radiator coolant, but with a substance as toxic as ethylene glycol I recommend it.

Survival Tips

Following is a collection of miscellaneous tips and advice to help you avoid common mistakes.

Never try to conserve water through abstinence. Some desert travelers have been found dead from thirst with a half-full canteen strapped to their sides. Heat exhaustion and stroke can hit quickly, rendering a victim unconscious without warning. When that happens things can only get worse, and the individual who loses consciousness in the midday sun may never wake up again. The best place to carry water is in the stomach; a canteen should only be used to carry water that won't fit there.

Carrying two pebbles in the mouth is an old Apache method of warding off thirst. The pebbles fool the mouth into thinking that it has something edible, which causes the saliva to flow and keeps the mouth from drying out. Chewing gum will do the same thing, but since sugar or artificial sweeteners increase feelings of thirst, gum used to keep the mouth moist should be chewed well after the flavor is gone. But remember, placing an object in the mouth will only help to stave off the feeling of thirst—it does nothing to replenish water lost through perspiration, and it will not prevent dehydration.

Night travel is always recommended when traveling on foot through arid country. Even the slightest physical exertion in temperatures that routinely top 100 degrees Fahrenheit will cause you to perspire heavily, and noticeably and seriously deplete your body's precious water supply. Conversely, the cloudless sky will allow the heat of the day to dissipate rapidly after sunset, with temperatures sometimes falling to the freezing mark. Since the nights are too cold to sleep and the days too hot to walk, the survivalist should always travel at night, holing up in a shady spot during the day.

If shade isn't available, it can be created. In Chapter 2 we briefly covered suspending a space blanket or poncho between two poles lean-to fashion to create a shaded sleeping area. This is probably the best hot-weather shelter in open desert, but erecting it requires a minimum of two poles. In sand or rock, where only low scrub can survive, these may be impossible to come by. When that's the case, a shaded shelter can be created by finding or excavating a shallow, body-length trench in the ground or between two rock outcroppings and stretching the space blanket shiny side up across it. The ends on either side of the trench can be held in place by weighting them with rocks or just burying them in the sand. Both ends of the finished shelter should be left open to allow the circulation of as much air as possible. The reflective surface of the space blanket will throw back a large portion of the sun's heat and the area under the shelter will remain about ten degrees cooler then the outside. The shelter will also stick out like a sore thumb to any plane passing within five miles.

A survivalist traveling through barren country will want to carry as much water with him as possible, and he'll want to make the most of any water holes he encounters on his journey back to civilization. For this reason I recommend having two canteens in the survival kit. Additional water can be carried in makeshift canteens, the number and type of which are limited only by imagination and available resources. Perhaps the best emergency canteen is the resealable soft drink bottle. Ordinary screw-cap jars make good emergency canteens too. Plastic bags will also work, but since few of these are watertight, the best way to carry water in them is to fill them with saturated cloth, paper or foam rubber from a vehicle's seats. The absorbent material will retain water while the plastic bag will help to keep it from evaporating. A small drinking hole can be poked through the bag near its top and the water recovered simply by squeezing trapped water from the contents and into the mouth.

When you come upon a water hole, stream, or any other body of water in hot, arid country, never lie on your belly to drink from it, and absolutely never throw yourself into the water with the wild abandon depicted in Hollywood movies. A sudden cooling of the body after exposing it to hours of heat and dehydration can cause a state of shock severe enough to cause unconsciousness. It's one of life's bitter ironies that people dying of thirst in the desert have found water only to drown in it. The safest way of drinking directly from a waterhole or stream is to kneel and use a cupped hand or canteen cup to raise it to the mouth.

Coyotes and jackrabbits are the most numerous mammals in barren country. Rabbits and most reptiles can obtain sufficient moisture from their food to live, but coyotes need to drink regularly, usually in the early morning and late afternoon. If one were to follow a fresh set of coyote tracks for a mile or two in these conditions, he might very well be rewarded with a waterhole. Thirsty animals can smell water for long distances, and the survivalist traveling with a horse, burro, or dog can find water simply by giving his animal its head and following. But keep in mind that some desert waterholes contain toxic levels of alkalai. Use the solar still to purify any suspicious water before drinking it.

Rain is still a safe source of drinking water that the desert survivalist especially will want to make the most of. The efficiency with which he can collect raindrops will be maximized by using a space blanket or sheet of plastic to channel as many of them as possible into his canteen. Suspend all four corners of the plastic about two feet above the ground by tying them to stakes, shrubs or anything else high enough. With a sharp stick or knife, poke a small hole through the center of the sheet and position the canteen mouth directly below it on the ground. The sheet will sag in the middle under the weight of accumulated raindrops, forming a puddle that will drain downward through the puncture in a steady stream. With this method, even a quick downpour will be sufficient to fill the canteen.

five

FOOD

Food has always been first on the list of priorities of primitive peoples. It was the one element of their lives that was most often unpredictable and always subject to the whims of nature. Ritual dances and other ceremonies were conducted to appeal to the spirits responsible for bringing in the buffalo, creating rain, or initiating the spawning run of migratory fish. But appealing to the spirits wasn't all that effective, so it was the duty of every member of the tribe to be opportunistic hunters and/or gatherers. Many of the methods employed by the Indians to take wild game, fish, and fowl were so effective that they've been outlawed in the United States and Canada, but both of these countries recognize the right to harvest food in an emergency.

Common Edible Plants

Wild plants are generally the most dependable food source. The majority of nutrients necessary to sustain human life can be obtained from plants alone, but as the Indians and mountain men of old were painfully aware, meat is also important in a balanced diet. Most plants are edible in terms of toxicity, but some of those that are considered edible are neither palatable nor digestible. And some of those that are very nutritious and digestible also taste terrible. This section will cover only those plants that are easily recognized, widespread, nutritious, and tolerable to the human taste buds. Plants that have a short growing season, are limited to specific areas, or require boiling in several changes of water to remove their toxins won't be mentioned here. Mushrooms will be entirely ignored because they contribute little in the way of nutrition and are sometimes difficult to recognize, and certain species are downright lethal. The wild vegetables covered in this book represent only a small fraction of all edible wild plants. For those who want to include a more comprehensive catalog of wild plants in their survival kit, I recommend the Reader's Digest book, *North American Wildlife* and *Edible Wild Plants*, by Oliver Perry Medsger.

Reindeer Moss (*Cladina rangiferina*) is an easily recognizable member of the lichen family common to the northern United States, Alaska, and nearly all of Canada. Reindeer moss is only one of many species of lichen (hybrid plants that are half algae, half fungus) found throughout the world. Most of these are not only edible (after boiling) but contain nearly 100 percent of the nutrition required to keep a human alive and healthy in the wilderness. Many a stranded woodsman or explorer has survived a prolonged stay in the wilderness by eating these lowly plants. The most famous case occurred during the winter of 1943, when a group of Norwegian commandos was dropped into Nazi-held territory and forced to subsist on a diet of reindeer moss for months at a time between Allied airdrops. Reindeer moss is not at all tasty, but its many other qualities rate it as one of the best natural survival foods in the world.

REINDEER MOSS (*CLADINA RANGIFERINA*)

Found in open areas in northern regions all over the world. Member of Lichen Family. Grows from two to four inches tall. Color ranges from gray to green to blue. Dry and crunchy when dehydrated. Contains stimulant, antibiotic, protein, sugar, and a laxative when eaten raw. Usually grows in thick clusters or "carpets."

Reindeer moss is easy to recognize. It prefers sandy, open meadows and fields where it grows in carpet-like masses of dull blue, green, or gray that may extend for several yards in all directions. Individual plants will range from two to four inches high. During dry weather these carpets will be brittle and crunchy underfoot, changing quickly to a spongy mass in the lightest rain.

Reindeer moss and other lichens should always be cooked before eating because many of them contain a potent laxative that is destroyed by boiling or baking. Other ingredients that are not destroyed by cooking include a high sugar content, most vitamins, most minerals, and a broad-spectrum antibiotic similar to penicillin. Canadian "sourdoughs" are reported to make a stimulating tea by boiling a strong concentration of crushed reindeer moss in water. I've tried this tea and the lightheaded feeling it gave me was anything but stimulating.

Reindeer moss can be prepared as a food by simply boiling it for a few minutes and then eating it right out of the canteen cup, but the most common method of preparation is to boil it, mash it into a paste, and bake it into cakes on a hot rock. Alaskan Eskimoes are also known to eat reindeer moss as-is from the first stomach of freshly killed caribou. This dish is known as "Eskimo salad" and although I haven't tried it, I'm sure it isn't much of an improvement on the taste of baked lichen cakes.

Plantains are one of the most common "weeds" on the North American continent, and at least one species is found everywhere from the tip of Alaska to Central America. Common plantain (*Plantago major*) can be found growing in swamps, fields, manicured lawns, gravel driveways, and through cracks in sidewalks. This tenacious plant is the bane of modern gardeners and suburbanites because it can be cut to the ground only to reappear again within forty-eight hours. Ironically, it was once highly prized as a food plant. The leaves are richer in vitamin, A, C, and iron than spinach, and its seedpods contain several of the B vitamins.

Plantains are easily recognizeable anywhere they grow, and the entire plant may be eaten raw or boiled as a potherb. The

COMMON PLANTAIN (*PLANTAGO MAJOR*)

Grows two to twenty inches tall and looks similar to small rhubarb plant. Leaves tasty and nutritious, richer in iron and vitamins A and C than spinach. Seedpods are green with pinkish flowers, and are a good source of vitamin B. Grows everywhere from fields to cracks in city sidewalks. In bloom from april to October. Found all over American Continent.

texture is a bit tough and the leaves are stringy, so I recommend boiling the plant until tender. The taste is a bit bland, but not at all unpleasant. Plantains can be found everywhere from April until the winter snows cover them.

Queen Anne's Lace (*Daucus carota*) is the most common member of the wild carrot family. Its tall stems, with their frilly white umbels (many-lobed flowerheads), can be seen in every open field, pasture, and abandoned lot on the continent from May through October. The vertical leaves are frilly and even a bit scraggly, and the center of the umbel is dotted with a single, dark-colored flower. There is some danger of confusing this plant with the

QUEEN ANNE'S LACE (*DAUCUS CAROTA*)

Found in open meadows and fields. Grows up to 5 feet tall with white umbel flowers. Edible white taproot smells strongly of carrots. Very similar to the highly toxic Hemlock plant except for no carrot odor.

very similar, very toxic poison hemlock (*Conium maculatum*), but positive identification can be made simply by smelling the root. Queen Anne's lace and its relatives have a strong odor of carrots, whole hemlock does not.

Queen Anne's lace is best when gathered before it flowers, because by the time it blossoms the edible taproot will have become woody and very tough. In the early stage of growth the plant very much resembles a garden carrot, with a white taproot rather than orange. It will still be a bit tough and chewy, but it's edible and tasty. As a flavoring for stew or soups, the taproot can be used at all stages of the plant's development. Queen Anne's lace can be found from late April until the first winter snows.

Watercress (*Nasturtium officinale*) is the survivalist's best, and sometimes only, source of fresh greens in the winter. It grows in running fresh water almost everywhere in the world, and when snow covers the ground it will be the only green plant found in streams, rivers, and springs. In summer it can be found growing in thick green carpets that sometimes completely choke smaller streams. The small clusters of tiny four-petaled flowers bloom from March to November, rising vertically from the surface of the water on slender stalks and ranging in color from white to light pink.

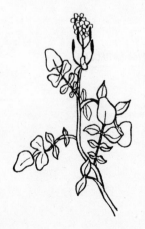

WATERCRESS ENTRY (*NASTURTIUM OFFICINALE*)

Vine-like growth forms up to 10 feet long. Small, white four-petal flowers from March to November. Leaves are dark, shiny green, and divided into many leaflets. May be found in nearly any fresh water and stream at all times of the year, sometimes growing so densely as to resemble a solid mass. Often creep up on streambanks during the summer months. Should be thoroughly washed before eating.

Watercress has long been sold commercially as a low-calorie, vitamin-rich vegetable. Eaten raw, it has a tangy, pungent taste faintly reminiscent of horseradish, but since its vine-like growth form is a favored browsing place for parasite-carrying freshwater snails, I recommend that it be boiled before eating, or at least washed very thoroughly.

Cattails are nature's own smorgasbord and no survivalist need ever go hungry where these distinctive plants grow. Both the common cattail (*Typha latifolia*) and its slightly smaller relative, the narrowleaf cattail (*Typha augustifolia*) are an excellent source of wild food every month of the year. The tall, reed-like growth form of the cattail is familiar to most folks. They can be found growing in ditches, marshes, along streambanks, and almost anywhere else fresh water is found in North America.

The edible parts of the cattail plant are the root, the core of the young shoots, the immature green seedhead, and the thick yellow pollen from the spike atop the mature brown seedhead. Young shoots begin to sprout in early spring, sometimes pushing their way upward through unmelted snow. These can be snapped off just below the surface of the ground and the white core eaten raw after the stringy green leaves have been stripped away, or they can be boiled briefly to make a dish known as "Russian

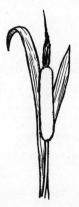

COMMON CATTAIL (*TYPHA LATIFOLIA*)

Grows two to ten feet tall. In bloom from May to July. Has starchy edible root. Tender young shoots may be prepared by boiling or steaming like asparagus. Basal portion of stem may be eaten raw. Found in marshes, ditches, and along lakeshores and riverbanks. Leaves inedible, but may be woven into mats, blankets, and other items.

asparagus." The raw shoots are crispy and pleasant to eat, with a flavor that I can only describe as a cross between celery and water chestnuts.

The thick rootstocks of the cattail can be eaten either raw or boiled any time of the year. Some authorities have likened them to potatoes, but the similarity is limited to the fact that both contain starch. Cattail roots have a tough outer "bark" and a fibrous texture that bears little resemblance to the soft, fleshy potato with which we're all familiar. They are nutritious and palatable, although some may find the very high starch content mildly objectionable. Probably the best way to prepare them as a survival food is to use the same method as the Indians of old. They simply roasted the roots over a bed of hot coals until tender and chewed them, swallowing the starch and spitting out the inedible parts.

The green cigar-shaped seedhead was also eaten by the American Indians, who roasted or boiled them and then ate the cooked fruits like corn-on-the-cob. I've eaten these cooked either way and am not overly fond of the taste—which is slightly bitter—or the texture. The flesh is reportedly nutritious and digestible.

From May to July the male cattail plants produce large pollen-bearing spikes that sit atop the mature seedhead. As a survival food this pollen is both nutritious and very palatable. Large amounts of it can be gathered in a relatively short time by using a stick to knock the powder into a bush hat, canteen cup or similar container. When enough of the powder has been collected it can be mixed with a little water, stirred into a thick batter, and made into "pollen cookies" by spreading the mixture thinly over a hot rock or mess tin. A couple of turtle or bird eggs will enhance both the taste and texture.

Violets (family *Viola*) are an abundant, nutritious, and very palatable wild vegetable that should never be overlooked by anyone facing a survival situation in warm weather. There are more than sixty species growing in North America. Some have violet flowers,

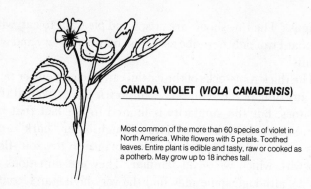

CANADA VIOLET (*VIOLA CANADENSIS*)

Most common of the more than 60 species of violet in North America. White flowers with 5 petals. Toothed leaves. Entire plant is edible and tasty, raw or cooked as a potherb. May grow up to 18 inches tall.

some white, some yellow, and at least one species is pink. Regardless of the color of the flower, all species are edible, although the downy yellow violet may cause a mild case of diarrhea if eaten raw.

The most common species of violet in the forests of the United States and Canada are the common blue violet (*Viola sororia*), arrowleaf Violet (*Viola sagittata*), white violet (*Viola macloskeyi*), Canada violet (*Viola canadensis*), and downy yellow violet (*Viola pubescens*). The leaves are generally heart shaped but in a few cases resemble the scraggly multi-lobed leaves of the toxic buttercup. For this reason I recommend avoiding any violet that doesn't have heart-shaped leaves, especially if no flower is present. All violets in bloom will have five petals, and the two top petals will almost always stand vertically together above the other three. The bottom-most petal will point downward and will be marked by a number of ray-like lines spreading from the center of the flower in all directions. Flowers will always stand above the plant on their own stems, and each of the leaf stems will support only one leaf. Plant sizes vary with the species but may range from two to twelve inches tall. Most violets can be found growing almost anywhere, but all of them prefer moist or even wet soil. The white violet especially prefers swamps and marshes.

The entire violet plant may be eaten raw or boiled as a potherb, and the flowers are a good, if meager, source of raw

COMMON BURDOCK (*ARCTIUM MINUS*)

Nearly all parts edible—starchy taproot, tender young leaves, stems, and basil leafstalks that can be peeled and eaten raw or boiled. In bloom from July to October. Found in fields, vacant lots, pastures, and nearly any other open place. Looks very much like rhubarb before flowering. Found all over American continent.

sugar. The uncooked leaves and stems have a very mild, pleasant taste that's hard to distinguish from raw lettuce.

Common Burdock (*Arctium minus*) is a plant familiar to most of us; only Alaska and the extreme northern territories of Canada are beyond the range of this hardy weed. A thornless relative of the thistles, burdock grows to a height of five feet and is common to fields, abandoned lots, open woods, and streambanks throughout its range. Immature plants very much resemble a hairy form of rhubarb plant, and the purple-tufted burs of the mature growth can be seen rising above the surrounding grasses in open fields.

The leaves, stems, and root of the burdock plant are all edible, but only the root is actually palatable. Some survival authorities have claimed that the fleshy stems can be peeled and boiled or eaten raw, but my own experience is that even with the bitter rind removed, the taste is sufficient to cause an involuntary grimace. The young leaves are also said to be good as a potherb, but these too are very bitter. The large rootstock is only slightly bitter after it has been peeled and boiled, and this is the part best suited as a survival food. Were it not for the burdock plant's large size and great abundance I would overlook it entirely.

Fishing

Fish are easily obtained throughout North America. Eating their flesh provides proteins and important vitamins, although most species are a bit light on calories. All fish are edible and nearly all of them are tasty, including carp, suckers, chubs, and other species that are generally snubbed by sportsmen.

Handfishing is a skill that the majority of woodsmen seem to think orginated in Hollywood and can only be performed by actors using drugged fish. The truth is that catching fish with only one's hands is not only possible but quite easy if it's done correctly.

Suckers (family *Catostomidae*) are the most abundant prey for the hand fisherman, especially in the early spring from late March to early May, when most species migrate into small streams and tributaries to spawn. These fish will scatter at your approach, hiding under sunken logs, stumps, and hollow streambanks. Hidden thus, the fish feel safe and will generally remain in their hiding place. To catch them, the "fisherman" simply reaches into the hiding place with his open hand held palm up and close to the stream bottom. With his fingers and thumb spread wide, he feels for the belly of his prey. When he feels the belly of the fish touch his open palm, he closes his fingers and thumb like pincers around the fish's body and removes it from the water. That's all there is to it. This method will also work with trout, bass, and other fish small enough to be held with one hand so long as the hiding places are dark or the fishing is done at night.

I learned the hand-fishing technique from a group of good ol' boys I encountered on a small Lake Michigan tributary early one spring. Like most folks I've passed this skill along to since then, I was very skeptical. But after seeing how easily these fellows plucked fish from under streambanks and logs, I wasted no time in joining them in the cold water. I caught fifteen suckers that day with only my hand, and only missed on one attempt.

Spearfishing is an age-old method that has been used with great effectiveness for thousands of years. Its efficiency can be maximized through the use of a tined steel spearhead. Some prefer a fishing spearhead, but I recommend carrying one or even two of the smaller four-tine frog spearheads because they can be used on frogs and other fish that are too small to be taken easily with the fishing spearhead. Considering its low price, versatility, and portability, the frog spearhead may at times be the most functional food-gathering tool in the survival kit.

Assembling the spearhead into a working tool requires a long, straight green sapling (my preferences are maple and cedar), and a small eyescrew that's just large enough to fit through the small hole on the side of the spearhead shank. The shaft should be at least five feet long, as straight as possible, and just slightly larger in diameter than the opening in the spearhead. The end of the shaft will have to be whittled down to fit into the spearhead tightly, even to the point of spreading the split in the shank apart a bit. Finally, twist the eyescrew into the shaft through the round hole in the side of the shank to keep the spearhead from coming loose when lifting a wriggling fish from the water.

The classic picture of the spearfisherman usually depicts him standing ankle-deep in the water with spear raised and poised to drive into the flesh of unsuspecting prey, a striking pose that is neither efficient nor effective. All species of fish are very much alert to danger from above, and the silhouette of a poised fisherman is usually enough to keep them out of range. Conversely, a spearhead held just above the water seems not to bother them at all if it's held still and moved only slowly into striking position. The most successful spearfisherman will always take advantge of natural cover by concealing himself behind stumps, bushes, or other permanent camouflage. A forked stick driven into the ground will help to support and aim the spear while he waits.

An observant spearfisherman may also notice open holes adjacent to the roots of large trees and stumps where running water has cut a channel under the bank. By getting on his hands and knees and peering into these holes with hands held at either side of his head to block out sunlight, he may also see that there are fish hiding there. These fish can be speared through the hole, providing it's large enough. Taking one fish in this manner will cause the others to scatter, but be patient, because most of them will return to the same hiding place, unable to comprehend danger in a place that has always provided safety.

Fish can also be speared through the ice of frozen lakes, although fishing with a line is probably the best method of taking perch, smelt, and pike in the winter. Many inland lakes contain very large northern pike, pickerel, and muskellenge, and these will often venture into shallow water to prey upon smaller fish. The stranded woodsman who chops a hole two feet in diameter through the ice in shallow water (five feet, maximum) and is willing to wait will eventually be rewarded with a passing fish. "Chumming" the water with a smaller fish cut into pieces will help to attract other hungry fish within spear range. A thick seat of pine boughs over the ice will provide insulation from the cold, and using a poncho or blanket to block out daylight will make it easier to see the bottom of the lake through the hole in the ice.

Large pike are also easy prey from May to mid-June, when they swim into shallow streams, rivers, and even tiny creeks to spawn. During this time they will sometimes appear to simply ignore the spearfisherman. But don't be too greedy; pike are very powerful fish that can exceed five feet in length, and their thrashing can twist even the stoutest spear tines into a pretzel. Always be certain that the fish is small enough to be handled by the spear.

Nearly everyone is familiar with fishing with a pole, and it offers two distinct advantages over fishing with a handline. First, it allows the fisherman to reach out from shore and place his bait precisely where he wants it without exposing his silhouette and spooking the fish. Secondly, a long, springy pole helps to tire a hard-fighting fish by preventing it from getting a solid pull, while allowing the angler more control during the contest.

Pole selection should be matched to the size and strength of the quarry. A long, thin pole of red-osier dogwood or river willow is sufficient for bluegill and most other small fish, while a heavier pole made from cedar, ash, or even maple is best for suckers, smallmouth bass, and other large fish. Twenty-pound-test monofilament line is usually more than enough to land any fish you might hook. Unlike sportfishermen, the survivalist is less interested in the fight than the food.

Trigger lines are an effective and simple method of hooking several fish at a time without being present when the fish bite. I learned this technique from a Chippewa Indian more than twenty years ago and have used it often to provide a meal of brook trout, perch, and other small fish. I've used it to take fish weighing more than a pound, but don't recommend it for larger fish.

The principle behind the trigger line is similar to that of a spring snare used to take rabbits and other small animals, except in this case the trap is laid in the water. It begins with a relatively short (no more than three feet) springy green pole chosen to match the size and weight of the intended prey. (A cedar branch with a base diameter of one inch is usually ideal for brook trout.) Sink the butt end of the pole vertically into the earth to a depth of about six inches. Secure the fishing line to the opposite, narrower end and bait the hook with a worm, grub, or insect. Then drive a wooden stake into the ground on the upstream side of the pole, about six inches away from it. Cut a notch into the side of the stake facing the pole and bend the end of the pole toward the

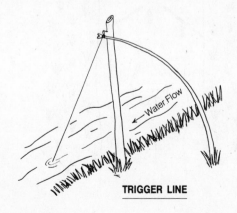

TRIGGER LINE

water and wedge it into the notch. The trigger line is now cocked and ready to spring at the first tug from a fish. When the fish bites it will flex the pole and pull it free of the retaining notch, causing it to spring back with enough force to set the hook deeply. To be as effective as possible, wedge the pole into the notch (or under a nearby cut-off tree branch) in such a way that even the slightest pull will snap it free into its upright position. This takes a bit of practice, but once the trigger line has been mastered it can be counted on to provide a fish dinner. A dozen trigger lines can be set along a streambank or lakeshore in under an hour. I suggest setting them at night just before turning in.

Trapping fish is another American Indian method that produces good results, especially in shallow streams. The most common method is to create a fence across the stream by shoving

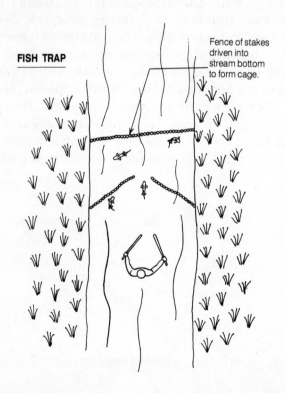

FISH TRAP

Fence of stakes driven into stream bottom to form cage.

a row of close-set stakes into the bottom, with a gap of no more than an inch between each stake. The fence is left open in the middle for a distance of about two feet to allow fish to swim through. About five feet upstream of this door, set a second, solid fence, with no holes for the fish to swim through. When both of these fences have been completed one can either wait for fish to swim into the trap or actively flush them into it by starting a hundred yards or so downstream and wading back toward the trap, poking a spear into hollow banks and any other places where fish might be hiding. If you plan on driving the fish before you, construct the first fence so that it angles inward on either side of the doorway in a funnel shape.

Not all fish will allow themselves to be driven upstream, and some will shoot past you in the opposite direction. Most, however, will flee toward the trap. You get best results when the fish are incited to blind panic by a lot of splashing and noise. When you reach the doorway of the trap, simply block it with your legs and spear the fish, or close the trap with another row of stakes and keep the fish alive until they're needed. The fish trap is especially useful for taking migrating fish during a spawning run; salmon run in late fall, suckers in early spring, trout and pike in late spring.

Bowfishing has been practiced by primitive peoples the world over since about the fifteenth century, and possibly even earlier in some parts of the world. Since fishing spears were handmade, often elaborate, and always difficult to replace, they were never thrown but rather used to pin the fish to the bottom until it stopped struggling (also good advice for the modern survivalist). When the fish were difficult to stalk or remained out of spear range the fisherman would shoot them with his fishing bow and arrows.

The fishing bow and its arrows are simple to construct. The bow consists of nothing more than a straight green sapling of springy wood such as cedar or willow. The ideal bow stave is approximately five feet long by two inches in diameter. It need not have a powerful draw, as the body of a fish is much easier to skewer than that of most mammals. It also doesn't have to be elaborately whittled, shaved, fashioned, or formed the way some recommend. A simple straight green sapling will do the job every bit as well as the more meticulously crafted bows, but with a lot less time and effort.

Bowstrings are also simple for the well-prepared. Instead of twisting plant fibers or cutting rawhide and sinew, use a nylon bootlace, jacket drawstring, or just snip off a six-foot length of the much stronger nylon cord from a survival kit. For sheer strength, durability, and resistance to rot, no natural cordage can compare to man-made nylon string or parachute cord. The bowstring is attached to the bow by cutting a small notch across each end of the stave, about two inches in from the ends. Tie a looped slipknot in one end of the bowstring, fit the string into the notch and pull it tight. Turn the bowstave over so that the attached end is resting against the ground and flex it until there's a gap of about ten inches between the string and the center of the bow. With the bow flexed thus, fit the loose end of the bowstring into the notch, wrap it twice around the stave and tie it off snugly. The bow is ready for use.

Fishing arrows are different from hunting arrows in that they need no fletching and are much longer. The ideal candidate for a fishing arrow is a young green willow or dogwood sapling about a half-inch in diameter at the base and four feet in length. Arrowshafts must be as straight as possible to prevent them from deflecting in the water. Notch the butt end slightly across the cut end to accommodate the bowstring, and sharpen the opposite end to a point, then notch two to three small barbs to help keep the arrow from pulling free after penetration. The ends of the green arrowshafts can be hardened by charring them slightly over a hot bed of coals. Like the fishing bow, fishing arrows don't have to be complex or meticulously crafted to be effective. Some recommend using cattail or mullein stems as arrows because they typically grow very straight. My own experience is that these are too fragile for fishing arrows.

In use, the fishing bow and arrow operates pretty much the same as a conventional hunting bow, the only real difference being the distance from hunter to target. Fishing arrows are much longer than hunting arrows, allowing the hunter to place the tip of his arrow close to his target, almost to the point of touching it while holding the bow at full draw. Ideally, the distance from the tip of the arrow to the target should never exceed twelve inches. Holding the tip of the arrow underwater will help to compensate for refraction.

Whenever possible, shoot for the fish's head for a quick kill. Even so, the fish will seldom just roll over and die, but will probably head for cover with a splash. A ten-foot length of cord tied securely to the arrowshaft and anchored on the opposite end to a sapling will keep smaller fish from escaping into deep water. For larger fish like spawning salmon, tie the cord to a float made of light-colored dry wood. (This should only be employed on streams where the fish can't escape to deep water.)

Firearm fishing is an effective method for taking large migrating fish such as salmon, trout or pike. These big fish often travel through shallow streams where their backs are exposed above water. The hungry survivalist who has a .22 rifle can simply station himself at one of these shallows and shoot them as they pass. A bullet through the spine or head is sufficient to kill the largest fish. It may take off, but it won't go far. Firearm fishing is limited to larger fish in shallow water because water is probably the best bullet stopper in creation; no caliber can penetrate more than a few inches before its energy is completely absorbed.

Spawning salmon can also be taken with only the survivalist's belt knife. This method is surprisingly effective, and while my success with it has been limited to salmon, it might also prove successful on other large fish under the right circumstances. Salmon can be found resting under banks, logs, and stumps, much the same as suckers, except that these fish are far too large to be caught in the hand. The hunter should hold his knife underwater as he slowly, deliberately approaches the fish, knife point forward and cutting edge up. When the fish is within striking distance, drive the point home just behind the head and pull upward hard, as though trying to raise the fish out of the water. This will generally not raise the fish from the water, but it will mortally wound the animal. When the struggling fish frees itself and speeds off down the stream, watch where it goes. It won't travel far before turning belly-up and flopping weakly. All that remains is to pluck it from the water.

Long-bodied fish can also be snared with a wire loop made from fencing wire, a wire saw, or snare wire. This is an old farmer's trick used mainly to take spawning salmon, pike, and other large fish in shallow water. Cross a six-foot lenth of stiff, smooth fence wire into a loop of about one foot in diameter, and close it by twisting the end into a loose slipknot. Wrap and twist the opposite end of the wire to the end of a stout sapling about six feet long and two inches in diameter. There should be approximately one foot of wire between the end of the sapling and the slipknot of the loop.

In practice the sapling is held horizontally at its midsection with the loop hanging straight down. When the fisherman spots a resting fish he dips the open loop into the water just in front of the fish's head. (All movements should be slow and smooth to avoid spooking the prey.) When the loop is directly in line with the fish's head, move it back and position it around the fish's midsection. With the body of the fish halfway through the loop, bring the forward end of the sapling straight up with a hard jerk. The wire loop will tighten around the fish's midsection and bite into its flesh with an inescapable grip. All that remains is for the fisherman to lever the struggling fish out of the water and onto shore. The fish snare can also be used to take smaller, lighter fish like suckers and smallmouth bass, but the stiffness of the wire must match the weight of the fish to be effective. The wire should be flexible enough for the loop to tighten quickly and easily around the prey's body, yet stiff enough to hold the loop open and steady as it passes over the fish's head.

Now the fish must be prepared for cooking. Cleaning fish in a survival situation is just a bit different from what most fisherman are used to. The animal should be gutted by slicing it open from anus to gills and removing the entrails, but the head, skin, and scales should be left in place. Leaving the skin in place will help to contain the valuable fat during cooking. The cheeks of most fish also contain sizable chunks of meat that shouldn't be overlooked, while the brains are rich in fat. Most folks will wrinkle their noses at the thought of eating fish brains, but sucker brains are considered a springtime delicacy by Canadian Indians of the far north. Someone whose body is in need of fat will find himself eating them with relish.

Fish caught in the wild must never be eaten raw, as many of them carry parasitic organisms in their tissues. The easiest way of cooking fish in the wild is to spear them on a spit and cook them over a low, hot fire. Larger fish are spitted through the body at the tail and then again through one eye, with the spit finally exiting through the mouth. This will bend the fish into a U shape and help it to cook more evenly. Smaller fish can be hung over the fire by spitting them through one gill and out the mouth. When the meat turns white with obvious layers in it and the skin separates easily from the flesh, it's ready to eat.

Fish flesh decays quickly in comparison to other types of meat, which makes it difficult to store or carry as a survival ration. Raw or cooked, fish meat becomes inedible after about two days in warm weather, but this period can be extended to as much as five days by smoking or salting the meat.

To prepare any fish for smoking, remove the entrails, spit it through both gills, and make an incision on the back down to the spine from head to tail. The cut down the back will help the fish to dry more evenly. Larger fish like salmon may require two or three similar cuts along the sides of the body.

Fish and other meats can be smoked over a low, open, and very smoky fire, but best results are obtained when a teepee-type frame is built around the firepit and covered with an outer layer of leafy green branches, packed snow, or even a wet blanket. Keep in mind that smoked fish are not actually cooked but dried by warm, smoky air (this does kill any parasites that might be in the flesh). The fire inside the smoker should always be kept low and very smoky by feeding it green "sweet" woods like apple, maple, poplar, or birch. Never use any pine or cedar for smoking or even cooking over an open fire because it will give the meat a distinct taste of turpentine. The fire should be allowed to draw only enough air inside the smoker to keep it alive.

Smoked fish are done when the skin separates easily from the meat, which should be firm and white. The meat in turn will separate from the bones in chunks. The drier the fish, the longer it will remain edible, but overdrying will make the meat tough and difficult to separate from the bones. Smoking generally requires about twenty-four hours, a bit less with thinly-sliced red meat, and the survivalist should be prepared to stay in one place for a day or so if he wants to use this method to preserve meat for the trail.

Other Marine Animals

Fish aren't the only marine food in most parts of the continent. Crayfish (family *Astacidae*) are common to most of North America. These miniature lobsters reach an adult length of five inches and can be used as food from spring until they hibernate in the muddy bottom in the fall. The easiest way to gather crayfish is to dangle a small piece of fish, clam, or even a worm on a fishhook in front of the underwater crevices, rocks, and holes in which they hide during daylight. The crayfish will dart out to grab the morsel in a powerful claw, so tenaciously that it will usually not be able to release its grip before the hunter pulls it from the water. These nocturnal crustaceans can also be gathered at night by blinding them with a flashlight in the shallow water where they feed and then simply plucking them off the bottom.

Crayfish are cooked by dropping them alive into boiling water, which kills them instantly. The crayfish is ready to eat in five minutes, and like the larger lobster, their shells will turn a brilliant red or orange. And also like the lobster, the meat in the tail and claws is edible. In fact, it's delicious. Cajun Indians also suck the salty juices from the body after the tail has been twisted off. Some may wrinkle their noses at sucking juices from the animal's internal organs, but the taste is worth trying.

Most turtles are a tasty source of meat if they're large enough to be worth the effort. The most common edible turtle is the aquatic snapping turtle (*Chelydra serpentina*), found nearly everywhere in the continental U.S. east of Colorado.

Snappers are predatory animals that often bury themselves in the mud at the bottom of a stream or pond to lie in wait for unwary prey, which they capture in powerful jaws. The survivalist walking along a streambank will be able to spot lurking snappers by watching for a sudden cloud of silt at the bottom near the bank. A survival knife or stick used to probe the surrounding mud will help to locate the shallowly-buried turtle and pry it from the mud. But be careful; snapping turtles are surprisingly docile in the water, but when threatened on land they become very aggressive and are quite capable of inflicting a bloody bite or even breaking a finger.

Like all cold-blooded creatures, snapping turtles in northern climes are true hibernators and bury themselves in the mud shallows of streams and ponds to sleep away the cold weather months. From late fall to early spring turtles can be gathered as food using the same probing method described above.

Before the turtle can be prepared as foot it must first be killed. This is best accomplished by holding a stick in front of the animal's nose. When it extends its neck to clamp its jaws around the sticky, simply lop the head off with a survival knife, hatchet, or machete. This will dispatch the animal quickly and mercifully.

Cleaning a turtle in preparation for cooking is simple. The upper shell (carapace) and lower shell (plastron) can be separated from one another by using a sharp knife to cut through the skin between the legs where the two join. Extend these cuts down each leg to the foot and peel the skin away from them, cutting both skin and feet free at the joint. The legs are the meatiest part of the turtle, followed by the back muscles. When the plastron and carapace have been separated, cut all four legs free and strip the meat from the spine with a small, sharp knife. The meat should be washed thoroughly to help lessen the strong "wild" taste. The meat can be cooked on a spit or cut into small pieces and boiled with rice.

Snapping turtle eggs should never be passed up as survival food. Female snappers can be seen laying as many as forty eggs the size of ping-pong balls in a loosely excavated hole on the banks of lakes, ponds, streams, and rivers from early May to June. A patch of freshly loosened soil near water during this period is a sure sign that there are eggs below it. Fresh snapper eggs are every bit as tasty as chicken eggs and they can be prepared in any way a chicken egg can. But don't hesitate in digging them up or you may have to compete with a skunk or raccoon, both of which are notorious egg stealers.

Frogs (family *Rana*) are an abundant, tasty, and easily obtainable source of food throughout North America during the summer months. The bullfrog (*Rana catesbeiana*) is the largest American frog, with a body length of up to eight inches. They are found in roughly half of the U.S. but almost none of Canada. Other frogs, like the pickerel frog, leopard frog, and green frog also have meaty hind legs that are smaller but just as tasty as bullfrog legs.

Frogs can be gathered by walking along a streambank with a small stick in hand. Those that are hiding in the grass will leap into the water at your approach—and then immediately stick their heads out of the water to get a look at what it was that frightened them. A whack on the head will kill the curious amphibians instantly. Pond- and marsh-dwelling frogs can be speared, although this practice is most effective at night when a flashlight is used to blind the creatures.

But probably the most effective daylight method for gathering frogs is the hook-and-line method. This "frog-fishing" technique uses a long slender pole to dangle an impaled fly or bee in front of the hungry frog. Fooled into thinking that it has an easy meal within reach, the frog will lash out with its long tongue and draw the insect into its mouth, fishhook and all. All that remains is to pull the hooked animal to shore and kill it with a sharp rap on the head.

It's good that frogs are so abundant, as it takes about a dozen bullfrogs or as many as twenty of the smaller leopard frogs to make a good meal. Even the largest frog has little meat on its body aside from the hind legs. Remove these from the body of the dead animal by cutting each of them off at the pelvic joint, then remove the skin by peeling it backward toward the foot like a banana and cutting it off at the lowest joint. The peeled legs can then be cooked on a very small spit, but they taste best when fried in a mess-kit skillet, with a little water added to keep them from sticking to the pan.

Birds

Birds are edible, tasty, and abundant everywhere in any season. There are a number of ways to take them but some are specific to certain seasons, some are specific to certain species, and a few methods are too time consuming to be of value to the traveling woodsman. The best tool for obtaining fresh fowl (or any small game for that matter) in an emergency is a .22 caliber rifle with a telescopic sight and with at least 100 rounds of Long Rifle ammunition. An accurate, familiar rifle can give a hunter a tremendous edge over even the best primitive weapon by allowing him to precisely place his shots from distances that will take his prey by surprise.

Ducks and geese are among the most valuable of birds to the survivalist because of their large size and fatty meat. Both are abundant on almost any waterway from early spring to late fall, when they migrate to southern regions. But be warned: both of these birds are tough and bullet placement must be exact. A bullet through the breast will almost certainly kill the bird, but usually not before it can fly out of sight. I recommend aiming for the head or neck. Shooting for either of these vital areas will either kill the bird on the spot or miss it completely.

When using any projectile weapon to take waterfowl, whether it be a rifle, slingshot, or bow and arrow, always try to stalk the quarry from high ground overlooking the waterway. Ducks and geese have very keen eyesight, but like most animals they seldom look up for danger. A stealthy hunter can work himself into position for a clean shot on swimming waterfowl if he can remain above the birds as they swim past.

Waterfowl are also easy prey for the bow and arrow. The hunter who's well camouflaged with green twigs and grasses attached to his clothing can lie in wait on a high bank and ambush the birds as they swim past, and usually at ranges of less than thirty feet. In the north, early morning and late afternoon are prime times to catch meandering ducks and geese, from spring to fall.

The American wild turkey is the largest gamebird on the continent. Once nearly decimated over much of its range, the turkey is now found in only the southern and eastern United States and Mexico. There are none in Canada.

Those who hunt turkeys using conventional methods will tell us that these birds are wily and hard to bag. But animals that have been very nearly hunted or trapped to extinction are typically not all that intelligent, and from my own experience the turkey is no exception. The Indians hunted these big birds by simply following them and shooting them as the flock foraged for food. Turkeys can fly only a short distance, so those that fly away can be easily located and stalked a second or even third time. Turkeys are not migratory, and those caught in deep, fluffy snow can even be run down on foot. At night they roost in large trees to avoid predators. A head shot is the best bet for the hunter armed with a .22 rifle; those using the bow and arrow should aim for the breast and trail the wounded bird until it can be caught. Turkeys are gregarious and flocks are active from daylight to dusk. Turkey eggs can be found in large leafy nests on the ground from late April to early May. (See information on Turkey tracks later in this chapter).

Ruffed grouse (partridges) are smaller than turkeys but their behavior patterns are similar. During the spring mating season these birds—especially the males—can be downright stupid. From May to June breeding males advertise their presence by standing on a log or stump and drumming their wings to attract a mate. The sound is very much like that of a chainsaw engine that refuses to start. As a boy I regularly potted these birds with only a slingshot. If one is careful and quiet, partridge can be stalked very closely. And like turkeys, they may fly when startled, but will usually land after traveling only a hundred yards or so.

Birds other than those recognized as sporting fowl can also be eaten. A few, like the merganser, loon, and seagull have a very strong, musky taste that makes them so unpalatable as to be inedible, but most others are both edible and tasty. In ancient Rome, candied sparrows were considered a delicacy fit for royalty. Blackbirds, crows, and any number of other birds are also fair game, especially for those armed with a .22 rifle. A slingshot or bows and arrows are better than nothing, but the smallbore rifle will gather more birds—and more food, for that matter—than any other weapon.

Should the survivalist be without a working firearm or ammunition, he can resort to the old Indian trick of laying a circle of loose footsnares around an area where birds congregate to feed or roost for the night. These snares are best made from heavy nylon string, but loops made from doubled twenty-pound-test monofilament will also work for ducks and other smaller birds. Each noose should be two to four inches in diameter, depending on the size of the bird, and closed with a loose double slipknot that will become tighter when the bird pulls against it. Suspending one end of the loop above the ground an inch or so with blades of grass will increase the probability of the prey stepping through it.

FOOT SNARE FOR BIRDS

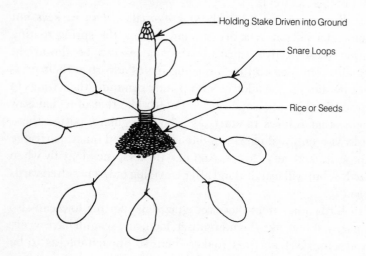

Holding Stake Driven into Ground

Snare Loops

Rice or Seeds

When one of them does, the low, clumsy walking gait and large feet common to birds will cause the loop to tighten around its ankle. The double slipknot will ensure that the noose only becomes tighter the harder the bird pulls to get free. Fasten the opposite end of each snare to a convenient sapling or a wooden stake driven into the ground. These too should be tied off using a slipknot, and the stake should be grooved around its circumference to prevent the snare cords from slipping off as the birds attempt to fly away. A small pile of rice, sunflower seeds, grass seeds, or almost any available wild seed will help lure birds into the trap.

The next step is one of those unpleasantries of survival. When the woodsman sees that a bird is caught by the foot, he should waste no time in rushing forward to dispatch it. Large birds like turkeys and geese can land powerful blows with their wings, and turkeys are armed with dagger-like spurs on the backs of their legs. The best way to avoid being bludgeoned, bitten, or stabbed is to use a stout green sapling of at least two feet in length to kill the bird with a hard blow to the head. This method is fast, practical, and merciful.

Preparing the bird for cooking is as simple as lopping off the head, making an incision from the anus through the breastbone to the open neck, and pulling out the entrails. I don't recommend plucking the bird because, like the Indians, I've found it to be more of a bother than it's worth. Skinning is much easier and less time consuming. The larger wing and tail feathers will have to be plucked, but the rest will be stripped off when the skin is removed. Skinning a bird is a lot like peeling an orange; just find a loose end around the gut incision and pull it free of the flesh. Birds have thin skin and it almost certainly won't come off in one piece, but it comes off easily with only the fingers, and skinning a bird takes half the time of plucking. When the skinned bird has been washed in clean water it can be roasted on a spit or cut up and boiled with a handful of rice to make a nutritious, filling meal.

An even simpler method is to wash out the eviscerated body cavity and then coat the outside of the unskinned bird with an inch of thick, wet mud. Then set the mud-covered carcass belly-down on a bed of red-hot coals and cover it with about three inches of additional coals. After about forty-five minutes the mud will have become a hard, crusty shell. At this point the bird can be removed from the fire and peeled like a boiled egg. The skin and feathers will adhere to the baked mud and when it's all been removed what will be left will be a juicy, succulent meal of baked wildfowl.

Mammals

Fur-bearing animals are an important source of meat protein and vital fat. Any animal that can get past the taste buds is edible. This section deals with those that are most abundant in North America.

The Porcupine (*Erethizon dorsatum*) has long been held in esteem by Indians and white woodsmen, both of whom consider this lowly animal to be a gift from God to the lost or injured. In most of the United States and nearly all of Canada this easily recognized vegetarian is prevalent enough to be considered common, and even a nuisance in some areas. Ironically, this spiny, dimwitted mammal is well protected against attack from any predator except man, and on the ground it's about the only animal a man can catch.

Porky can be hunted at any time of the day every month of the year, but they're mostly active at night during the warmer months. In a snowlocked forest the slow, rather clumsy animals will often find a large food tree and stay there for several days to several weeks. A number of freshly clipped sprigs on the ground below a white pine indicates that a porcupine was and may still be feeding in it.

Porcupines also den in upright hollow trees at all times of the year. These can be identified by a large number of dark brown pellet-shaped feces at the base. The pellets average one inch in length and about three-eighths of an inch in diameter. The texture of older, dried pellets will be fibrous and woody, reflecting the diet of the animal that deposited them. Older denning trees will have a large pile of scat (feces) around their base, which is sometimes where the door to the den is located. But the animals aren't found exclusively in dens and can often be spotted during the daylight hours sleeping on a large branch in tall oaks, maples, and poplars.

Porcupines invariably climb up into a denning tree unless the door is located high above the ground. Inside, they spend the daylight hours sleeping on a hard platform made from their own compacted feces. They can often be spotted as they peer curiously from a lofty den opening. If this happens, don't shoot the animal, because whether wounded or dead it will certainly fall back inside onto the sleeping platform, where it will remain until the tree falls. The best way to bag a denned porcupine is to approach the den from its blind side in late afternoon, take up a station behind cover about thirty yards away and wait until the unsuspecting critter emerges in the evening to feed.

Porcupines have a well-deserved reputation for being hard to kill. Their primitive brains just don't register the shock of a bullet wound the way more highly developed animals do, and even multiple hits with 12-gauge buckshot often won't be sufficient to kill a porcupine quickly.

But a single head shot from a .22 rifle will kill the animal instantly. I recommend head shots for all wild game taken in a survival situation, but especially for the porcupine. A porcupine caught on the ground can be dispatched with equal mercy by hitting it hard across the nose with a stout club. The quills can't be thrown, but a porky can inflict serious injury by swinging its spiny tail, so always keep well out of range. Information on porcupine and other animal tracks can be found on pages 128–129.

Rabbits and hares are a plentiful source of fresh meat everywhere on the North American continent. All of them except the plains jackrabbit make their homes in swamps, brush, or some other type of heavy cover. Only seldom do rabbits actually excavate their burrows, preferring instead to take shelter under brush piles, fallen logs, or in the abandoned dens of other animals. Winter scats are spherical and approximately three-eighths of an inch in diameter, although like most herbivores, rabbits feeding on green foods will often deposit soft, shapeless droppings.

Some sporthunters scoff at the idea of hunting the speedy rabbit with a .22, but it's a lot easier than it might at first appear. Rabbits and hares are largely dependent upon camouflage to conceal them from predators because, fast as they are, the lynx, coyote, and bobcat can outrun them. The survivalist who jumps a hiding bunny in heavy brush or the deep sawgrass of a swamp should immediately freeze and follow the fleeing rabbit with his eyes. It won't often run more than fifty yards and will stop to conceal itself in the first cover it finds. But human eyesight is superior to that of the rabbit or its four-footed enemies, and the survivalist will likely be able to spot the motionless animal, especially if his rifle is equipped with telescopic sights.

TRACKS

Wild Turkey (*Meleagris Gallopavo*)

Very Large, standing 3 to 4 feet high. Roosts in trees and feeds on the ground. Diet consists of insects, berries, nuts, and seeds. Found in deciduous forests and wooded bottomlands. Nests on ground in spring.

Canada Goose (*Branta Canadensis*)

22 to 40 inches tall. Usually found near water, but may occasionally be found in corn or grain fields, especially in fall and spring. Nests on elevated ground near water in spring.

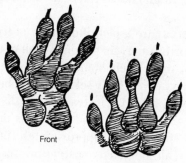

Front

Hind

Woodchuck or Groundhog (*Marmota Monax*)

14 to 20 inches long, excluding tail. Burrows underground. Hibernates in winter. Found in open forests, forest edges, and fields.

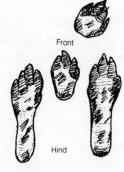

Front

Hind

Snowshoe Jackrabbit (*Lepus americanus*)

15 to 19 inches long. Brown in summer, coat turns white in winter. Active mostly at night, but can often be found standing motionless in brush or deep grass during the day. Found nearly everywhere, but seems to prefer swamps and thick brushy areas. Toes can spread very wide in snow.

TRACKS

Front

Whitetail Deer (*Odocoilus virginianus*)

4 to 6 feet long. Up to 4 feet tall at shoulder, but usually less. Long tail white on underside, raises when alarmed. Active early morning, midday, and early to late evening. Feeds mainly at night in open fields and meadows. Beds down in swamps and other thick cover during the day. Eyesight poor, hearing and small acute. "Yards up" in winter, feeding on cedars and marsh grass when normal feeding areas are covered with snow.

Hind

Squirrel (*Family Sciurus*)

8 to 11 inches long, excluding tail. Found in oak, maple, and beech forests. Occasionally found in pines. Nests high in trees. Nests are a leafy mass lodged in branches. Active all year, but mostly in fall when nuts and acorns ripen.

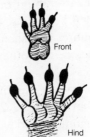

Front

Hind

Front

Porcupine (*Erethizon dorsatum*)

18 to 23 inches long, excluding tail. Mostly nocturnal, and may often be seen sleeping high up in a tree. Can be found in brushy areas and forests, but seems to prefer pines. Active all year.

Hind

Note: Tracks shown are as they might appear in mud or soft earth. Perfect tracks, such as those shown, are more often the exception than the rule. Track in snow may look different.

Squirrels There are several species of squirrel native to North America, and all of them are edible. The pine-dwelling red squirrel is smallest of these and is usually spurned by sport hunters, but the hungry survivalist can't afford to pass up any source of meat. Other species like gray or black squirrels prefer hardwoods such as oak, beech, or maple, because these large trees provide them with both food and shelter. All squirrels build leafy nests and sleeping platforms high in trees where they'll be safe from predators, but those of the larger squirrels are most obvious. Wintering squirrels will also nest in a convenient hollow tree.

Squirrels can be hunted either by sitting and waiting for them to come into the open, or by simply walking quietly and shooting them as they appear. Both methods are effective, but the traveling woodsman will probably opt for the latter. Squirrels are normally quite wary, but their downfall is their keen sense of curiosity and short attention span. The sitting hunter who shoots one has only to wait about fifteen minutes before the others simply forget he's there and go about their business.

Squirrels can be taken in a number of ways, including snaring, the slingshot, and the bow and arrow, but again the .22 rifle is best. These animals are masters of concealment and will often lie motionless on the opposite side of a branch or tree trunk where even a shotgun can't reach them. A scoped .22 will help to spot the hiding animals and allow the hunter to precisely place his shot. Squirrels often forget that they have a big bushy tail attached to their backsides and this is often what gives them away.

Raccoons (*Procyon lotor*) are prevalent and even overpopulated in the United States, Mexico, and southern Canada. The meat is quite palatable and some folks say it tastes like lamb, although I'm not one of them. The fat is not tasty, but it is rich, and the survivalist suffering from cramps and diarrhea caused by fat malnutrition will no doubt eat it with relish.

Raccoons are active mainly at night, but as a boy I took a great many of them during the day simply by walking quietly through the forest. During the winter they may sleep for several days at a time, but they're not true hibernators and can be seen out foraging for food every month of the year.

Once again the .22 rifle is the best tool for the job. A bow and arrow will also do, but the shooter should be prepared to defend himself because a wounded raccoon can be vicious and will likely attack. If this happens the animal must be clubbed dead before it can inflict the serious injury it's capable of creating with claws and fangs. Rifle shooters should always go for a head shot with raccoons.

The Beaver (*Castor canadensis*) is widespread throughout North America, even to the point of having pest status in some locations. This animal more than any other is responsible for the vast personal fortunes that were made during the eighteenth century, when the United States became one of the most powerful empires in history. The thick fur of Brother Beaver was also held in high esteem by the Indians, who valued the meat at least as much as the fur.

Beavers are remarkably well adapted aquatic rodents that can reach an adult weight in excess of 100 pounds, although sixty pounds is normal. They might be found living in any body of water, whether it be a lake or small creek, that has poplar, aspen, cottonwood, or birch growing along its shores. Although mostly nocturnal, beavers can usually be incited to leave their lodge during daylight if you tear a large hole in the dam and then hide nearby to wait for them to emerge. The animals react instinctively to the sound of rushing water and seem compelled to repair their dam regardless of risk. The Indian method of hunting them was simply to shoot the animals with arrows or bullets as they worked to repair the dam.

The Labrador Eskimos used a different technique: they blocked the entrance to the beaver lodge with stakes driven deeply into the mud and then tore through the roof of the lodge. It was a point of honor for the hunters to grab the big rodents by the hind feet and draw them into the open alive, but the survivalist who uses this method should headshoot the animal where it lies. If the lodge is occupied by more than one animal, clear the entrance to allow the others to escape before attempting to retrieve the dead beaver.

The whitetail deer (*Odocoileus virginianus*) is another animal that has been reduced to pest status in many areas. Its proliferation is largely due to civilized man's determined effort to wipe out its natural enemies, the wolf and the puma. Because of the deer's size, the survivalist should take a deer only out of desperation, when no other game is available. Even a yearling whitetail will yield about forty pounds of boneless meat, far too much to carry while walking through the wilderness. Much of it can be preserved through the same smoking method used for fish, but it's inevitable that the woodsman on the move will be forced to leave some behind.

Deer are strict vegetarians, and are especially fond of clover and alfalfa in wilderness areas. During the months when these plants are available the animals will emerge from their bedding areas in the thickets and swamps each evening to feed. Whitetails are largely nocturnal, but it isn't at all unusual to see several of them foraging in the middle of the day. When winter snows cover their normal foods, the deer will move in herds to a sheltered valley or swamp to feed on juniper and cedar foliage until spring. Deep winter snows are tough on whitetails but they can be a definite advantage to the stranded woodsman who must hunt them.

As poachers are well aware, the .22 is quite adequate for taking deer, but only in the steady hands of a skilled marksman. A mere head shot isn't always adequate; deer have been known to take a .22 bullet between the eyes and still run away because the projectile glanced off the animal's sloped forehead. The survivalist's primary target should always be the eye. If this is impossible, a quick knockdown can be had by shooting for the base of the skull or the meaty portion of the neck directly under the jaw. A shot through the ear is also quite effective. A single bullet will seldom be enough to kill the animal instantly, so be prepared to follow through with a killing shot at close range.

Before any of the aforementioned animals can be used as food they must first be skinned and gutted. If one has never skinned an animal before this can be a confusing and messy operation. But it doesn't have to be. The following method is simple, clean, and generic. It will work well with all four-footed animals, whatever their size or species. Since the porcupine is perhaps the most likely animal to be used as survival fare, and because it's the most difficult animal to skin, we'll consider it in the following example.

With this method, called "tube-skinning" by furriers, the hide is removed from the animal in one piece without opening the stomach cavity. Larger animals like deer, antelope, or wild pigs are most easily skinned by first hanging them upside down by the hind legs from a tree limb. This will keep the hind quarters spread wide apart and allow one to pull hard while removing the hide.

The first step is to make a cut around the circumference of the lowest joint of both of the animal's hind legs. These cuts are then connected by another cut that runs along the inside of each leg and across the anus. Always keep a porcupine on its back whenever possible during skinning because most of its quills are concentrated on the tail and the back; the belly is covered with wiry hairs, but not quills.

Next, strip the hide away from the hind legs and down toward the head as far as possible. Sever the tailbone with a twisting, pressing motion, but don't cut the tail free of the body. Grasp both hind feet, one in either hand, place the heel of one foot on top of the tail, and pull hard upward. With luck, the hide will peel down to the shoulders with a single stroke. If the tail pulls free of the body, just kick it aside and repeat the procedure by placing a heel on the freshly-loosened skin and pulling again. When the hide has been peeled inside-out down to the shoulders, free the front legs down to the paws and cut them free. Sever the neck in the same manner. The head and forepaws will remain attached to the hide, leaving you with a skinless carcass.

The last step is to remove the hind feet and eviscerate the animal. Remove the entrails by making an incision from the anus through the rib bones and down to the neck. This incision is best made by inserting the blade of the knife, cutting edge up, under the belly muscle and simply sliding it along. Cutting from the inside out in this way will lessen the chance of its puncturing the stomach, the contents of which emit such a strong odor that

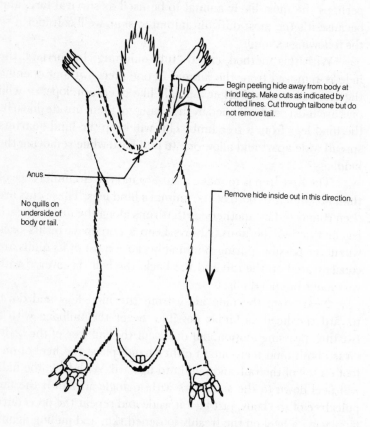

Begin peeling hide away from body at hind legs. Make cuts as indicated by dotted lines. Cut through tailbone but do not remove tail.

Anus

No quills on underside of body or tail.

Remove hide inside out in this direction.

**GENERIC TUBE-SKINNING METHOD
(PORCUPINE SHOWN)**

the uninitiated have been known to vomit. Split the pelvic bone by driving the blade through the anal canal.

When the stomach cavity has been opened from anus to neck, remove the entrails by pulling downward and outward from the chest cavity not on the organs themselves, but rather on the membrane to which they're attached. A knife will help to separate this thin, tough membrane from the ribs, taking all the innards with it.

If water is available, wash the cleaned carcass thoroughly and remove any pieces of organs that might still be attached, especially in the neck and the anal canal. If the stomach or other internal organs were punctured during cleaning, be sure to remove any of their contents from the meat, as well as any blood clots, and cut away any darkened, bruised portions; all of these will impart an unpleasant taste to the meat.

Cooking methods will vary with the size of the animal being prepared and the availability of other, complementary foods. In most cases the easiest and most practical method of cooking small game is simply to roast the carcass on a spit over a low fire. But if one has a bag of ordinary rice (nature's own freeze-dried food) in his kit, he can cut the meat into pieces and boil it with the rice. The addition of a few cattail shoots and some chopped Queen Anne's lace root will produce a good-tasting and highly nutritious meal. The same dish can be prepared using fish, fowl, reptiles, or even insects.

Snakes

Folks who haven't tried it—and who aren't hungry—will normally turn up their noses at the thought of eating a snake. The revulsion humans feel for snakes is a learned and purely psychological reaction impressed upon children by adults who learned it when *they* were children. Snakes are neither evil nor particularly aggressive, and their role in nature is infinitely more beneficial than the one played by man, the universal natural enemy.

All snakes are edible, nutritious, and palatable, regardless of species. Some are too small to be considered as a survival food because too many of them are required to make a meal, but any individual large enough to be worth the effort will provide tasty fare.

Nearly all of us have encountered snakes during walks and camping trips, but these are chance encounters for the most part, and when one is trying to stay alive in the wilderness it's never a good idea to depend on luck. A little information about the habits and requirements of any food animal goes a long way.

Snakes are cold-blooded creatures that because dormant in temperatures below fifty degrees Fahrenheit. In snow country they hibernate through the winter months and emerge again when temperatures rise in late spring. They can often be found sunning themselves on rocks and other open areas in the morning before the night chill has disappeared completely. In the heat of the day they take refuge under logs and rocks to prevent over-heating, and some desert snakes, like the sidewinder, will actually bury themselves in the sand. Snakes will also seek refuge in these same places to escape the cooling effects of rain. In the deep south, where temperatures remain warm through the night, many species will be active from dusk to dawn, but in the north, where nighttime temperatures can drop as much as fifty degrees after sunset, they tend to hide until dawn. All snakes are predators, and since most animals tend to gravitate toward water, swamps, lakes, and rivers are among the best places to hunt them.

Relatively few snakes are venomous, but nearly all of them will bite in their own defense, and some have enough teeth to make the experience an unpleasant one. With this in mind, the snake hunter should always be equipped with a stout pole of at least five feet in length. It need not be forked at the end, because the objective isn't to capture but to kill the animal. This is best accomplished by a single hard blow to the head. The hunter equipped with a .22 rifle can also take out large snakes from a distance with a head shot.

Skinning and cleaning a snake is quick and simple. First, remove the head and discard it, because even "dead" snakes have been known to bite. The action is purely reflexive, but that doesn't make any difference if the snake is venomous. For safety's sake I recommend kicking the heads of killed snakes directly into the campfire, venomous or not.

With the head removed, make an incision in the belly from the anus to the point where the head was taken off. Beginning at the top, use a finger to strip out the entrails; they should come out in one piece.

Next, find a loose flap of skin where the head was removed and work it free until the skin can be grasped firmly between the thumb and forefinger. The skin can then be stripped off in one piece. Wash the carcass thoroughly if sufficient fresh water is available.

Snake meat can be spitted and cooked over a low, open fire by weaving the spit in and out of the body to help hold it securely as it roasts. It can also be boiled and included in a dish of rice or wild vegetables, and if the animal is large enough it may also be sliced into thick, very tasty steaks.

Insects

Anyone who turns up their nose at the thought of eating snake meat will no doubt turn a deep shade of green at the mention of eating insects, but these six-legged animals have been a vitally important source of protein, carbohydrates, and fat all over the world since the beginning of time. Not only are they abundant in warm weather, but pound for pound insects contain more usable protein than beef liver. Again, the squeamishness most of us feel about eating insects is a learned reaction. After all, they're bugs and we've been taught that bugs are bad, crawly things.

In reality though, insects are an important food source that should not be overlooked by anyone in a survival situation. I'm not going to try to fool anyone by saying that insects are delicious (some really aren't too bad), but they are an easily gathered source of important nutrients, and eating them will keep one alive indefinitely.

Grasshoppers and locusts are probably the most easily recognized and abundant insects in the world. From the small one-inch North American grasshopper to the eight-inch giants of South America, these foliage-eating arthropods have been both the bane and boon of primitive peoples everywhere. When a swarm of locusts wiped out crops in ancient times, the locusts themselves became food.

Like all insects, grasshoppers and locusts should always be cooked before eating, because they are known to carry parasitic organisms. The American Indian method of gathering them usually consisted of setting a field or meadow afire at its edges and using the flames to drive the panicked insects—as well as rodents and other edible creatures—toward the center, where the heat would kill and cook them at the same time. The roasted insects were then gathered and eaten whole. In my experience, grasshoppers are quite palatable when roasted until crunchy, but they'll probably never make the menu of the world's finest restaurants.

Black ants and red ants are also valuable as a survival food. Their bodies contain concentrated raw sugar, proteins and formic acid, the latter of which gives them a sour but not unpleasant taste. Ant larvae are high in sugar and fat. These insects, their larvae, and their eggs are edible either raw or roasted, but taste better when roasted.

The task of gathering enough of the tiny insects to make a meal was simplified by the many tribes of American Indians who regularly ate them. A piece of fresh, sweet bark from a cedar, birch, or pine tree was placed on the ground next to an anthill. The sugar contained in the sap would attract the ants, which were then scraped off on a hot, flat rock to roast. After roasting the ants were either eaten whole or mashed into a sugary powder.

An alternate method used by some tribes was to knock the top off a large anthill and gather the insects by inserting long twigs into their midst. When the furious ants swarmed over the twig they were brushed off into a bag and left to die before roasting.

Grubs, especially the larvae of june beetles, are an excellent survival food because they consist almost entirely of fat. They can be found by digging in the earth, but are most abundant in rotting tree stumps and logs, even in winter. These are probably the most repulsive of edible insects for most people, so I recommend roasting them and swallowing them whole. The taste isn't bad, but the texture is enough to make many students of wilderness survival nauseous. It does no good to eat something if one is going to vomit.

All Bees, wasps, and hornets are edible if their stingers and the poison glands at the tip of the abdomen are removed. These insects are best gathered by walking through a field of wildflowers, swatting them to the earth, and then crushing them underfoot. The killed bees are then collected in a bag or similar container for roasting after their stingers have been cut off. Always use a knife, not the fingers, to remove stingers and poison sacs. A bee can still sting even in death. And never, ever try to assault a bee or hornet nest, not even for honey.

The Bow and Arrow

Like most everything else primitive, the survival bow and its arrows can't begin to compare to a modern hunting bow, either compound or recurve, for power and accuracy. As most bowhunters are well aware, the archery equipment of today is the most sophisticated and lethal in history. Modern archers can rightfully expect to score quick, accurate kills on game out to and beyond fifty yards, whereas even the most skilled Indian bowhunter of old knew in advance that he would have to take his shot at no more than fifty feet and then trail his animal until it bled to death. Still, the primitive bow and arrow can be an effective weapon if one keeps its inherent limitations in mind.

Some primitive survival instructors insist that the survival bow must be painstakingly selected from suitable wood, dried, formed, whittled, and wrapped with animal sinew before it can be used. This process requires about two weeks and is far too impactical to even be considered under actual survival conditions. In real life, the only function required of the bow is its ability to throw a pointed stick with enough force and accuracy to mortally wound the animal it strikes.

The ideal hunting-bow stave should be between five and six feet long and as straight as possible. The young green saplings of willow, locust, and cedar are among the best choices because of their flexibility, but maple will work in a pinch. (Pine is a poor

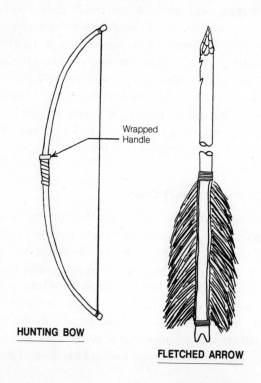

Wrapped Handle

HUNTING BOW

FLETCHED ARROW

choice because it will break rather than bend.) The stave should be at least an inch in diameter at the center and the ends should both be approximately the same diameter (at least three-quarters of an inch). A stave with a consistent diameter from end to end is ideal.

With the sawteeth of the survival knife, cut a shallow groove around the circumference of either end about an inch from the tip. These grooves will keep the string from slipping off when the bow is drawn. Parachute cord is probably the best material for a bowstring, but heavy nylon string or two bootlaces tied together with a square knot will also work very well. Attach the bowstring to one end of the stave with a slipknot, making sure that the string falls into the groove cut around its circumference.

Tie another slipknot in the opposite end of the string, which should be about eight inches shorter than the bowstave. Brace the tied end of the bowstave against the ground and flex it from the opposite end until the second slipknot can be placed over it. Again, make sure that the string falls into the groove around the bowstave's circumference. If the string length is correct, it will fall across the middle of the forearm between wrist and elbow when the bow is gripped around its middle.

Draw the bow carefully a few times to be certain that the string is securely attached and that the stave won't break under pressure. A comfortable non-slip handle can be fashioned by wrapping several turns of safety tape (mentioned in Chapter 1) around the center of the bow. A few additional turns of safety tape at the top of this handle will form a convenient arrow rest.

Workable arrows can be made from straight sticks or saplings—either green or dry—about three feet long and a half inch in diameter. Whittle the narrowest end to a sharp point; this will be sufficient to penetrate the bodies of smaller animals like raccoons and porcupines. If the arrowshaft is green, the tip can be hardened by charring it over hot coals. Cut a notch crosswise in the opposite end of the arrowshaft to accept the bowstring.

Unfletched arrows will work well to take game at ranges of up to thirty feet—far enough to take a porcupine out of a tree.

But accuracy is maximized by fletching the nock end of the arrow with the wing or tail feathers of almost any medium to large bird. Loose feathers can often be found along lakeshores and occasionally just lying on the ground in the woods. Split each feather down the middle to create two fletching feathers. These feathers are attached to the arrowshaft at either end, about one inch from the nock, by no more than three turns of safety tape or several turns of thin string. The strings and feathers can be glued securely to the shaft with melted pine pitch. Be sure to position the feathers in relationship to the nock so that they won't strike directly against the bow and deflect the arrow on release.

Each survival bow and its arrows are slightly unique, and no two will shoot exactly the same. Consistency is the key to accuracy, but so is practice. It helps to know if this particular bow shoots slightly to the right or left, or displays any other idiosyncrasies. I recommend shooting several arrows at a soft target such as an anthill to determine where the point of impact tends to be.

Snares

For the average person, strangling snares are the trademark of wilderness survival. But in reality, they have only limited usefulness for the traveling woodsman because the success of any snare or deadfall is wholly dependent on an animal falling prey to it. That doesn't happen as easily or as often as Hollywood might have us believe, not even under the best circumstances with the most skilled survivalist. The key to success is to set the snare in just the right location at the right time.

Well-worn animal trails are the most obvious places to set snares. The observant hunter will likely see many of these as he travels through the wilderness, especially near water. Bear in mind that most animals are nocturnal, and set as many snares as possible just before making camp for the night. To avoid spooking the prey unnecessarily, snares should be set a minimum of 100 yards from camp.

The "simple" snare is one of the easiest yet most productive of snares, largely because so many of them can be set so quickly. It consists of nothing more than a large loop closed with a slipknot and suspended over a game runway where any animal using the trail will encounter it. The strategy is to place it so the animal's head will pass through the loop as it walks along, but not its shoulders. Blades of grass or very small twigs can be positioned on either side to hold the loop open. When the prey animal's head passes through the snare, its shoulders and chest will push against the string, drawing the loop tighter as it walks along. When the snare begins to tighten around its neck the animal will almost always follow its natural instincts, which tell it to flee from danger. This is exactly what makes the simple snare so successful. Unable to comprehend what's holding it, the animal will usually lunge wildly until it strangles or breaks its own neck. (Occasionally it will bite through the snare cord and escape.)

When selecting a suitable cord for constructing the simple snare, keep in mind the approximate size of the animal it's being set for and the fact that it will fight hard to free itself. Ninety- or 100-pound-test fishing line or nylon string will be sufficient to hold small game up to thirty pounds. The cordage used for any snare should have a rated working load of at least twice the estimated body weight of the animal being snared.

The pencil snare is a classic spring snare. There are several other types of spring snare, but this one is without a doubt the one that will prove most useful to the survivalist because of its simplicity, reliability, and speed. It can be made in a variety of sizes to take everything from field mice to whitetails. Spring snares offer an advantage over the simple snare because the prey is physically lifted from the ground with enough force kill it quickly, and sometimes instantly. The animal has no opportunity to free itself by biting through the snare cord.

The design of the pencil snare is simple. The anchored end of the snare cord is tied securely to a springy sapling or tree branch, which must be bent over before the trigger can be locked in place. The opposite end of the cord is tied tightly around a

PENCIL SNARE

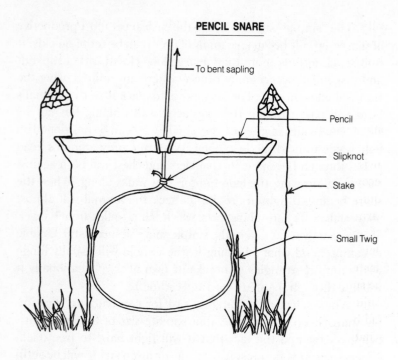

To bent sapling

Pencil

Slipknot

Stake

Small Twig

straight stick (the "pencil") about four inches above the snare loop. The pencil should be several inches longer than the intended prey is wide for reasons that will soon become apparent.

The pencil is used to hold the sapling or branch in the bent position by inserting it lengthwise between two notched stakes driven into the ground on either side of the trail. The notches in the stakes will hold either end of the pencil in place and prevent the upward pressure of the sapling from pulling it free. The snare noose hangs loose under the pencil and is held open with blades of grass or very small twigs placed to either side of it.

The most critical portion of any spring snare is its trigger, which in this case is the mating surfaces of the pencil and the notches in the stakes that hold it in place. The hold exerted by the notched stakes against the ends of the pencil needs to be as precarious as possible, so that the slightest pull against the noose will cause one end to slip free and allow the sapling to spring upward. This will help ensure that any animal that places its head through the noose and pulls even gently against it will be yanked upward with enough force to break its neck.

Most important of all, please always keep in mind that the only real difference between man and the other animals inhabiting this planet is his ability to think abstractly. Only man can envision a concept and then perform the tasks necessary for it to become a reality. Compared to our "lesser" cousins, man is poorly equipped to survive in the wilderness. We have no fur to keep us warm, no claws or functional teeth with which to fight and hunt, no sense of smell to speak of, and no natural hunting abilities. Only our ingenuity and intellect give us the ability to become masters of any situation. But these are more than enough, and the survivalist who uses the information contained in this book in conjunction with his own God-given intelligence will certainly find himself able to overcome any adversity he might encounter in nature.

Index